TEXTS THROUGH HISTORY

'A brilliant series – an absolute gift for teachers! This superb series makes clear tangible terminology and implicit meanings which to many students seem foreign. The books' methods and tactics are enjoyable and workable for both students and teachers, and the clear, evaluative and reflective models will enable students to obtain the necessary reflection in their own written responses.'

Kesner Ridge, Hagley Roman Catholic High School, Worcestershire, and Outstanding New Teacher 2002 (*The Guardian Teaching Awards*)

'This is the series we've all been waiting for! Tightly focused on the assessment objectives, these books provide an excellent aid to classroom teaching and self-study. Whether your school changes board or text, or decides to offer Literature and/or Language to 6th formers these books are still the tool that can make a real difference to results.'

Emmeline McChleery, Aylesford School, Warwick

Routledge A Level English Guides equip AS and A2 Level students with the skills they need to explore, evaluate, and enjoy English. What has – until now – been lacking for the revised English A Levels is a set of textbooks that equip students with the concepts, skills and knowledge they need to succeed in light of the way the exams are actually working. The *Routledge A Level English Guides* series fills this critical gap.

Books in the series are built around the various skills specified in the assessment objectives (AOs) for all AS and A2 Level English courses, and take into account how these AOs are being interpreted by the exam boards. Focusing on the AOs most relevant to their topic, the books help students to develop their knowledge and abilities through analysis of a wide range of texts and data. Each book also offers accessible **explanations**, **examples**, **exercises**, **summaries**, **suggested answers** and a **glossary of key terms**.

The series helps students to learn what is required of them and develop skills accordingly, while ensuring that English remains an exciting subject that students enjoy studying. The books are also an essential resource for teachers trying to create lessons which balance the demands of the exam boards with the more general skills and knowledge students need for the critical appreciation of English Language and Literature.

ROUTLEDGE A LEVEL ENGLISH GUIDES

About the Series Editor

Adrian Beard was Head of English at Gosforth High School, Newcastle upon Tyne. He now works at the University of Newcastle upon Tyne and is a Chief Examiner for AS and A2 Level English Literature. He is co-series editor of the Routledge Intertext series, and his publications include *Texts and Contexts*, *The Language of Politics*, and *The Language of Sport* (all for Routledge).

TITLES IN THE SERIES

The Language of Literature
Adrian Beard

How Texts Work
Adrian Beard

Language and Social Contexts
Amanda Coultas

Writing for Assessment
Angela Goddard

Original Writing
Sue Morkane

Transforming Texts
Shaun O'Toole

Texts through History
Adele Wills

TEXTS THROUGH HISTORY

Adele Wills

Routledge
Taylor & Francis Group

LONDON AND NEW YORK

First published 2004 by Routledge
11 New Fetter Lane, London EC4P 4EE

Simultaneously published in the USA and Canada
by Routledge
29 West 35th Street, New York, NY 10001

Routledge is an imprint of the Taylor & Francis Group

Typeset in Galliard by Keystroke, Jacaranda Lodge, Wolverhampton
Printed and bound in Great Britain by TJ International Ltd, Padstow, Cornwall

British Library Cataloguing in Publication Data
A catalogue record for this book is available from the British Library

Library of Congress Cataloging in Publication Data
Wills, Adele, 1963–
  Texts through history / Adele Wills.
    p. cm. – (Routledge A level English guides)
  Includes bibliographical references.
  1. History in literature. 2. History–Methodology. 3. Literature and
history. 4. Literature–History and criticism. 5. Historiography. I. Title.
II. Series.
  PN50 .W55 2004
  809′.93358–dc22

ISBN 0–415–31909–9 (hbk)
ISBN 0–415–31910–2 (pbk)

CONTENTS

PREFACE

ASSESSMENT OBJECTIVES

The AS/A2 specifications in English are governed by assessment objectives (or AOs) which break down each of the subjects into component parts and skills. These assessment objectives have been used to create the different modules which together form a sort of jigsaw puzzle. Different objectives are highlighted in different modules, but at the end of AS and again at the end of A2 each of the objectives has been given a roughly equal weighting.

All A Level English courses now require students to consider the way a text has been influenced by its context and this book will focus specifically on this topic. However, this cannot be discussed in isolation from the other assessment objectives. The main aim of the overall series is to develop the skills of critical analysis and, as a consequence, some cross-referencing to other assessment objectives will inevitably occur. For example, the chapter on genre will also consider aspects of form, language and structure. It is hoped, therefore, that in seeking to gain greater understanding of the ways to handle one assessment objective, you will inevitably extend your skills on a general level allowing you to develop into a more thoughtful, reflective and critical reader.

Each chapter contains a number of exercises. When the exercise introduces a new idea, there will usually be suggestions for answer immediately following. When the exercise checks to see if a point has been understood, suggestions for answer can be found at the back of the book.

Particular assessment objectives that are focused on in this book are:

English Literature

A01: in writing about literary texts, you must use appropriate terminology

A02: you must show knowledge and understanding of literary texts of different types and periods, exploring and commenting on relationships and comparisons between them

A03: you must show how writers' choices of form, structure and language shape meanings

A04: you must provide independent opinions and judgements, informed by different interpretations of literary texts by other readers

A05: you must look at contextual factors which affect the way texts are written, read and understood

English Language and Literature

A01: you must show knowledge and understanding of texts gained from the combined study of literary and non-literary texts

A02: in responding to literary and non-literary texts, you must distinguish, describe and interpret variation in meaning and form

A03: you must respond to and analyse texts, using literary and linguistic concepts and approaches

A04: you must show understanding of the ways contextual variation and choices of form, style and vocabulary shape the meanings of texts

A05: you must consider the ways attitudes and values are created and conveyed in speech and writing

English Language

A01: in writing about texts, you must use appropriate terminology

A03: you must show a systematic approach to analysing texts

A05: you must analyse the ways contextual factors affect the way texts are written, read and understood

ACKNOWLEDGEMENTS

The author would like to thank the following copyright holders for permission to reproduce material in this book:

Amanda Endewelt, *The Story behind Camelot*. Reprinted by courtesy of ABCNEWS.com

Page from The King Arthur Flour Company website reprinted with permission from The King Arthur Flour Company, Norwich, Vermont, USA.

Randall Wallace, *Braveheart* © Randall Wallace, 1995. Reprinted with permission of Penguin Books Ltd and with permission of International Creative Management, Inc.

Arthur Miller, *Death of a Salesman*. Reprinted with permission of International Creative Management, Inc. © Arthur Miller, 1949

Liz Lochhead, *Mary Queen of Scots Got Her Head Chopped Off* © Liz Lochhead 1987 *Dracula* © Liz Lochhead 1988. First published Penguin 1989. Reprinted with permission of Penguin Books Ltd.

Willy Russell, *Educating Rita*. Reprinted with permission of Methuen Publishing Ltd.

Magnet Kitchens advert reproduced with permission from Magnet Kitchens.

John Cleese, Graham Chapman, Terry Gilliam, Eric Idle, Terry Jones and Michael Palin, *Monty Python and the Holy Grail*. Reprinted with permission of Methuen Publishing Ltd.

Veetee Basmati Rice packaging reproduced with permission from Veetee Rice Ltd.

Edwin Morgan, 'Number 1 from Glasgow Sonnets' in *Collected Poems* © Carcanet Press Ltd, 1990.

The Heart of the Highland is taken from the Capercaillie album *Delirium* on Survival Records SURCD 015 www.capercaillie.co.uk The lyrics by John Saich are printed courtesy of Survival Music Sony/ATV Music Publishing (UK) Ltd.

Zadie Smith, *White Teeth* © Zadie Smith 2000. Reprinted with permission from Penguin Books Ltd.

With thanks to Rowenna Skidmore, Richard Huish College, Taunton, for the extract from the student essay in Chapter 6.

INTRODUCTORY PRINCIPLES   CHAPTER 1

This introductory chapter will consider why the historical, social and cultural contexts of both literary and non-literary texts are now so important for AS and A Level students across all three English specifications. It will also begin to formulate some guidelines for how this challenging area can be approached, initially illustrated through an extract from Ibsen's play *A Doll's House*. Later chapters will further develop the principles established here, ranging widely over different historical periods and incorporating both literary and non-literary examples.

Several key principles are at the heart of this book's critical approach:

- That the use of contextual factors to understand a text, either literary or non-literary, is an essentially intricate and multi-faceted endeavour
- That any attempt to access historical or cultural information and apply it to a text has to be tentative and provisional
- That, in spite of the provisos cited above, a text none the less cannot be read in isolation from its context and this initiates an ongoing cycle of critical readings and interpretations
- That none of these readings will be final or conclusive, but each will provide a different perspective from which to consider and interpret a text

WHY IS HISTORY IMPORTANT?

On one level, an understanding of the importance of historical, social and cultural contexts is essential for all A Level English students because these contexts form a central aspect of the assessment criteria for all three subjects. Thus, examiners will be looking for the way you use and discuss contextual issues, whether you are looking at literary or non-literary texts or a combination of both. The Preface gives more detail about this, but in essence all three specifications require students to have an understanding of the importance of contextual factors and, at A2 Level, to be able to evaluate them.

For example, you may have already encountered Shakespeare's play *Macbeth* as part of your earlier studies. On a straightforward level, this can be read as a play about a man who, through a series of negative influences, becomes corrupted in his search for power, leading to a story of bloodshed and murder. Shakespeare has skilfully managed to engage our interest in Macbeth as a character and, in reading or watching the play, we may be subject to a range of emotional responses: shock, horror, sympathy, etc. However, if we begin to analyse the play's historical context, then we can see that there are some more complicated ways of reading Shakespeare's intentions. The play was probably performed for the first time in Hampton Court before King James I in 1605 or 1606. The king would have been very pleased to witness the story of the downfall of a man who had murdered a king as he himself had recently survived a murder attempt in 1605 in what is now known as the Gunpowder Plot. It is also important to remember that in Shakespeare's time, most people believed in witches and thousands of women were tortured and executed in Europe because they were accused of witchcraft. James I in particular had a personal horror of witches. All of these historical issues give a different slant on our reading of the play and we begin to perceive this importance in a different way as a product of a particular society and set of values. Our response to the text becomes a complex process of interpretation whereby our own values and beliefs find themselves in dialogue with very different ones. Ultimately, this must give us a deeper understanding of our own historical identity and belief systems.

The assessment objectives, therefore, reflect an important theoretical change in recent approaches to studying English, changes that have fundamentally affected ways of reading. English is itself a relatively new academic discipline that only really established itself during the twentieth century. It was initially characterised by a belief in the importance of Literature as a work of art, complete in itself and capable of analysis solely on its own terms without reference to external factors. This became known as **practical criticism** and required students to engage in a process of close reading and analysis of language, seeking patterns and structures within the text. However, by the second half of the twentieth century, new critical approaches were becoming increasingly influential and, in conjunction with the rise of Linguistics which sought to develop the scientific study of language, the central ideas of practical criticism began to be challenged. It became unworkable to believe that a text could exist independent of its historical, social and cultural context.

During the 1980s, distinct critical schools developed which took particular approaches to the interpretation of literary texts. Some of these approaches can be summarised as follows:

- New historicist critics: who hold that the study of history is a primary preparation for interpreting any work of literature, although they agree that understanding history is never straightforward and the 'truth' can never objectively be known.
- Marxist and political/economic critics: who hold that every text reflects the political situation from which it was produced. They analyse texts for their representation of class issues, focusing on the way that power relations are presented, usually in terms of the exploitation of the poor by the rich. They often champion previously unknown working-class authors.

- Feminist critics: who are interested in the way texts represent the relations between men and women. These critics may take issue with the way women are shown to have little power in a male-dominated text; or they may want to challenge the books that are read and studied in the academic world by substituting female writers for accepted male authors. Considerable work has also been done on whether men and women use language differently, producing a range of theories.
- Post-colonial critics: who are interested in the way texts represent race and colonial issues. They analyse texts for the way that ethnic groups are represented, linking this, once again, to power relations. They may look, for example, at how far non-western characters are given a voice within a text or the words that are used to describe these characters; or, like both Marxist and feminist critics, they may challenge the limitations of what is often perceived as a white, male, middle-class tradition of literature (what is often known as the **canon**) aiming to provide non-western alternatives.
- Queer theory: this is the most recent of the critical schools, establishing itself in the 1990s. Critics from this school hold that our conventional definitions of sexuality are limited. Thus they seek to reinterpret both texts and personal identity from a gay, lesbian or bisexual perspective. Like so many of these critical perspectives, this school is often connected with the work of political activists who seek more power in society for gays and lesbians and object to stereotypical divisions of gender identity.
- Reader response critics: who hold that a text is not an object separate from the reader and that a text exists only when it is read. Thus, we can learn about a text by seeing how readers in different ages have responded to it. In one sense, all the above critical schools come under this broad heading and they have created communities of readers with common concerns and perspectives. However, reader response criticism also allows that the individual experiences, views and historical context of every reader will colour their response to a text.

All of these new approaches are intrinsically historical and give an indication of some of the ways in which history can be used to interpret texts. Many of these approaches also overlap and most of their followers are keen to explore the political ramifications of their readings and show an awareness of the relationship between literary texts and society.

So, our focus in this section has been 'Why is History Important'? The final answer must be that it encourages us, as critical readers, to see connections between textual productions and the real world. Texts are not independent entities, but productions from a particular person, or group of people, at a particular time and a fuller understanding of how they reflect real societies and ideas can allow us both to question and to develop our own belief systems and values. The example we discussed earlier from *Macbeth* illustrates this. Rather than simply being a play about the downfall of a particular man, the play in its historical context raises issues about kingship and sovereignty as well as the way women were perceived in

Jacobean society; we may respond from a Marxist or a feminist perspective to these issues. Texts **represent** a reality and the job of the critical reader is to **deconstruct** that representation. An understanding of a text's context in the broadest sense is a key way of doing this.

For further consideration of some of these issues, see Amanda Coultas's *Language and Social Contexts* in this series.

HOW DOES HISTORY SHAPE A TEXT?

A text may reflect its context in several ways and the examples and exercises in this book will explore these in greater detail. However, all of these factors fundamentally overlap and influence each other and so, although the following chapters reflect these divisions, they have, to an extent, been artificially imposed for the sake of clarity. Overall, an act of interpretation is a subtle, complex and continuous affair, which is extended with every new reading.

A text consists of several factors at the point of its production. These may be summarised as:

- The attitudes and values reflected in the text
- The text's genre
- The language used within the text

In addition, a text never stands on its own but is received by a community of readers with their own attitudes and values, thus producing another context:

- The text's critical reception

These will all now be considered in more detail, using a literary example to illustrate the basic principles.

ATTITUDES AND VALUES

In many ways, this is probably the hardest context to establish and the easiest to fall prey to crass generalisations. History is often divided into convenient periods which are seen to have dominant characteristics. Literature courses often reflect these divisions, particularly at university where modules are frequently called, for example, 'The Victorian Novel' or 'Elizabethan and Jacobean Drama'. These divisions are an essential way of giving clarity and focus to the subject and suggest, quite rightly, that texts written at certain times will have characteristics in common. However, this does not mean that everyone thought the same way. As we shall see later, a text is produced by an individual or a group of writers subject to a variety of influences. The process of interpreting and untangling this is never straightforward and, in some ways, the older the text, the harder it becomes. For example, it is easy to assume that seventeenth-century Jacobean society held a clear view about Jewish identity, usually expressed in what we would consider racist terms. However, this knowledge needs to be used carefully and tentatively when approaching plays such as Shakespeare's *The Merchant of Venice* – and our understanding could be further enhanced by comparing Shakespeare's text with his contemporary Christopher Marlowe's *The Jew of Malta*.

In a historical and social sense, attitudes and values are a reflection of the set of ideas that existed when the text was produced which would have affected the way people lived and thought. This is often referred to as **ideology**. This may affect key areas of people's lives such as:

- Gender – the roles that men and women were expected to fulfil within that society
- Class – the economic structure of that society and the way power was distributed on the basis of this
- Race – attitudes towards different ethnic groups or particular ideologies that may affect this such as imperialism

There may also be more specific issues that are reflected in texts from different periods. For example, critics have argued that Mary Shelley's familiarity with and understanding of the scientific debates and discoveries of her time, particularly Luigi Galvani's experiments on electricity, may have fundamentally influenced her 1818 novel *Frankenstein*.

Exercise 1

The following text is taken from the beginning of Henrik Ibsen's play *A Doll's House* which was first performed in Copenhagen in 1879. Read the extract carefully and then make a note of the attitudes and values that strike you as important in this text. In particular, focus on the representation of

- Gender: the roles that men and women appear to have had assigned to them and the way masculinity and femininity are represented
- Class: what clues the text gives us about the class of the people involved, based on wealth and style of living, and their relations with others.

ACT ONE

A comfortable room, furnished inexpensively, but with taste. In the back wall there are two doors; that to the right leads out to a hall, the other, to the left, leads to Helmer's study. Between them stands the piano. In the middle of the left-hand wall is a door, with a window on its nearer side. Near the window is a round table

continued

with armchairs and a small sofa. In the wall on the right-hand side, rather to the back, is a door, and farther forward on this wall there is a tiled stove with a couple of easy chairs and a rocking-chair in front of it. Between the door and the stove stands a little table. There are etchings on the walls, and there is a cabinet with china ornaments and other bric-à-brac, and a small bookcase with handsomely bound books. There is a carpet on the floor, and the stove is lit. It is a winter day.

[A bell rings in the hall outside, and a moment later the door is heard to open. Nora comes into the room, humming happily. She is in outdoor clothes, and is carrying an armful of parcels which she puts down on the table to the right. Through the hall door, which she has left open, can be seen a Porter; he is holding a Christmas tree and a hamper, and he gives them to the Maid who has opened the front door.]

NORA: Hide the Christmas tree properly, Helena. The children mustn't see it till this evening, when it's been decorated. [To the Porter, taking out her purse] How much is that?
PORTER: Fifty øre.
NORA: There's a krone. No, keep the change.

[The Porter thanks her and goes. Nora shuts the door and takes off her outdoor clothes, laughing quietly and happily to herself. Taking a bag of macaroons from her pocket, she eats one or two, then goes cautiously to her husband's door and listens.]

Yes, he's in.

[She starts humming again as she goes over to the table on the right.]

HELMER [from his study]: Is that my little skylark twittering out there?
NORA [busy opening the parcels]: It is.
HELMER: Scampering about like a little squirrel?
NORA: Yes.
HELMER: When did the squirrel get home?
NORA: Just this minute.

[She slips a bag of macaroons in her pocket and wipes her mouth.]

Come in here, Torvald, and you can see what I've bought.
HELMER: I'm busy!

[A moment later he opens the door and looks out, pen in hand.]

Did you say 'bought'? What, all that? Has my little featherbrain been out wasting money again?
NORA: But, Torvald, surely this year we can let ourselves go just a little bit? It's the first Christmas that we haven't had to economize.

HELMER:	Still, we mustn't waste money, you know.
NORA:	Oh, Torvald, surely we can waste a little now – just the teeniest bit? Now that you're going to earn a big salary, you'll have lots and lots of money.

Suggestions for Answer

Even without doing any research into the background to this text, you will very quickly have noticed several issues in relation to gender and class.

Ibsen introduces us to two main characters, one male and one female, a married couple. Both have clearly distinguished roles in this world; Nora Helmer is shown returning from a shopping trip and preparing the Christmas celebrations for her children while Torvald Helmer is in his study doing something that initially makes him too busy to come and see what Nora is doing. Note that Ibsen's extensive stage directions particularly specify that the study is Helmer's, thus drawing a physical distinction between the nature of men's work (that takes place in a study) and women's (primarily motherhood and home-making). The way Ibsen uses names in the playscript is also significant: the first name is used for the woman and the surname for the man, implying that men lead a more serious, professional and less intimate life than women.

Nora's character is also presented in a very specific way. As this is a play, we have both actions and language (**dialogue**) to construct our reading. Nora's actions suggest that she has a happy life. She enters 'humming happily', she gives a generous tip to the porter and she is described as 'laughing quietly and happily'. She also has a bag of macaroons which she is eating, although when her husband calls she hides them and wipes her mouth. The act of eating the sweets secretly makes her appear childish and immature but also raises an important issue of deception. Although a bag of macaroons may seem trivial, they could represent a lack of openness in her relationship with her husband and Ibsen may be commenting on the nature of marriage and its limitations in his 1879 society. The childlike impression is furthered by the way Torvald speaks to Nora using terms such as 'little skylark', 'little squirrel', and, rather disturbingly, 'little featherbrain'. Nora is linked to small, harmless creatures, emphasised by the repetition of the adjective 'little'.

Nora's speech to Torvald at this point is limited, simply answering his questions and the language makes it clear who holds power in this relationship. Torvald is also represented as knowledgeable about money and the importance of prudence, compared to Nora's generosity and propensity for wasting money (shown by the extravagant tip and the Christmas parcels). Their relationship could be described, in modern terms, as more akin to father/daughter than husband/wife and there is the suggestion of emotional immaturity. The play's title, *A Doll's House*, may support this reading. All of the critical analysis so far in this section would sit comfortably within the feminist school of critical reading.

A Marxist reading would focus more on class than gender, and, again, we can make some early suggestions. Ibsen has painstakingly described the appearance of the set and wants to represent a comfortable, tasteful middle-class domestic interior. We see that the house is 'furnished inexpensively', so the Helmers are clearly not wealthy, but the furniture is cosy and there are the signs of aesthetic appreciation in the 'etchings', the 'china ornaments', the 'piano' and the 'handsomely bound books'. The Helmers also keep a maid and can afford to tip the porter, yet they are not aristocratic characters with titles. We learn later that Torvald is going to 'earn a big salary' which tells us that they are not living on inherited wealth but on Torvald's earnings, the word 'salary' implying perhaps a professional career.

So how may this be linked to the play's historical context?

The play was first written in Norwegian and produced in Norway towards the end of the nineteenth century. At that time, women could not vote, had few property rights and were often little more than decorative servants. Marriage was an institution, a contract broken only by death, and a woman's prime role was to raise children with little involvement in public life. However, by the time Ibsen was writing this was beginning to be questioned and by the 1880s and 1890s a wave of feminist thinking began to sweep Europe.

Similarly, during the later part of the nineteenth century, social change was happening in relation to class. The Industrial Revolution had created a new middle class from wealth generated by industry in towns; this new social class began to challenge the old landowning aristocracy and created new jobs in areas such as banking and insurance (we later learn that Torvald works in a bank). Ibsen's play is set in a city where banking and law are respectable, lucrative occupations and where money and its acquisition become a prime focus of human activity.

So how does this help us to understand the play?

From our initial response to the play, we can see that Ibsen's setting and relation-ships do reflect his historical context in the way gender and class are represented. In particular, the fact that Ibsen has focused on a middle-class couple rather than on aristocratic society shows the rise to prominence of this group of people at this particular time, a change that resulted from a specific set of economic issues.

However, Ibsen was also an individual within this society and would have his own values and attitudes that he chooses to express through the medium of his play. To understand that he was writing against a background of the rise of feminist thinking must lead us to approach the play with this in mind. Ibsen's play may represent a response, or responses, to these issues. It is significant that Ibsen has chosen to focus on the central female character (the stage is focused on her space while the male domain is off-stage) so we can expect some consideration of the role of women within his society as Ibsen sees it.

THE INDIVIDUAL WITHIN HISTORY

So, we have already started to position this text within its historical and social context. However, the important concept to grasp here is that a text has been produced by an individual or a group of people within that context and this author (whether singular or plural) has a viewpoint on these issues that they wish to convey. Thus, texts do not simply reflect this reality but *engage* in some way with this reality and often stage conflicts to illustrate their exploration of specific ideas. An author may be at odds with their society or may endorse its values; this will be reflected in the text. It is not enough to know that Mary Shelley was familiar with the scientific debates of her day; critics have interpreted *Frankenstein* as an expression of Mary Shelley's deep unease at the progress of science and the likely consequences of man's interference with the natural order.

Exercise 2

Read the following Text A and Text B from Ibsen's *Notes for the Tragedy of Modern Times* published in 1878 and then relate these back to your initial reading of the opening of *A Doll's House*.

- How do these extracts extend your first suggestions concerning the representation of gender in the play?

Text A

A woman cannot be herself in contemporary society, it is an exclusively male society with laws drafted by men, and with counsel and judges who judge feminine conduct from the male point of view.

Text B

These women of the modern age, mistreated as daughters, as sisters, as wives, not educated according to their talents, debarred from following their missions, deprived of their inheritance, embittered in mind – these are the ones who supply the mothers for the new generation. What will be the result?

Suggestions for Answer

We can see from these quotations that Ibsen was essentially a man of his time, engaged with and challenging contemporary issues. While a study of the play's historical context shows us that the representation of gender and class reflects the state of society at that time, we can also begin to understand Ibsen's response to this. Perhaps, we could argue, Ibsen has chosen to represent Nora and Torvald's relationship as so extreme because he wants to show how unhealthy and limiting this view of marriage is, since the balance of power is so unequal. We may also have some initial ideas about Ibsen's view of middle-class society and its values – although you will need to read more than just the beginning of the play to develop these ideas.

We could also bring in biographical issues at this point: Ibsen was the oldest surviving son of Knud Ibsen, a prosperous merchant whose financial failure in 1835 brought the family to bankruptcy and the very edge of respectable society. How is this likely to have left Ibsen himself feeling about the demands of 'respectable society' and the importance of money?

GENRE

Texts also exist within a history of writing, that is, in a cultural context. This again assumes that no text is produced in isolation, but looks at the other types of *cultural production* which existed both before and contemporaneously with that text. Every **genre** has a set of conventions and expectations, although every new text will extend and challenge these conventions. Issues of language, structure and form will be relevant here as they are the building blocks of genre. Seeing texts as part of a group, or several groups, can help to establish a fuller reading. (For a more detailed examination of the role of language in creating genre, you could also refer to Adrian Beard's *The Language of Literature* in this series.)

There are several generic issues raised by Ibsen's play that establish his place as a revolutionary writer. In 1872, the Danish critic Georg Brandes attacked Scandinavian writers for dealing only with the past. Ibsen took note of this and began to write plays that dealt with modern problems. Ibsen is often credited with the development of this new kind of play, called a **problem play,** that deals with modern social and moral issues. The main characters belong to the middle or lower classes and the action focuses on domestic and family life. Ibsen often referred to his play as a modern **tragedy**. Tragedy goes right back to the Ancient Greeks and it has been defined and redefined as a genre over the years (see chapter 5 for a more detailed exploration of this). What Ibsen did was take a main hero who was neither male nor aristocratic but a middle-class woman in ordinary domestic surroundings. Ibsen also wrote in prose as opposed to poetry to emphasise his focus on everyday concerns and, as we have seen, described his settings in minute detail to establish the reality of both place and character. His settings also became **symbolic**: if you read the play, notice the significance of the Christmas tree and the way it changes as the play progresses.

This information about the play, therefore, looks at a broader context of literary works and is not solely dependent on the text itself. This does not mean that a detailed knowledge of the text is irrelevant; but it does mean that this is not sufficient for a full reading and understanding of a text.

LANGUAGE CHANGE

This is itself a significant area of study, particularly for students of English Language/Literature and English Language. Clearly, there are links with genre, but you also have to be aware that language itself changes over time and this will be reflected in the text. This may be shown in a variety of ways:

- The choice of vocabulary or **lexis**: words change in meaning and spelling over the years and you have to be sure that the meaning you are ascribing to the text is the one in use at the time. The *Oxford English Dictionary* or dictionaries of **etymology** give further information on the development of individual words. Use of **colloquialisms, dialect** or **slang** may reflect particular periods.
- **Grammatical** or **syntactical** changes: the age of texts can be reflected by sentence length or by **archaic** constructions.
- **Phonological** or sound changes: these changes can affect **rhyme** sounds or could reflect either region or social class of a speaker in terms of **accent**.

READER RESPONSE

The final stage in making sense of a text focuses on the *reception* of the text or the reader response. Every time a text is read by a new reader, then a new act of interpretation is taking place and these readings also become part of the nature of that text. Older texts that are frequently studied in academic circles (these texts are often known as the canon) are likely to have a dense critical heritage and each of these readings will, in turn, reflect its own context. Modern readings may have been produced from within the critical schools that we considered at the beginning of the chapter. Texts are also never popular for all times; the group of Jacobean writers known as the metaphysical poets only really became popular in the twentieth century as a result of an influential essay and a collection of their verse published in 1921. Thus, you need to consider readings produced by other readers, but also to understand the context of these readings if you are to be able to evaluate them.

Ibsen was a writer fundamentally at odds with his society and it is probably no surprise to learn that his work immediately caused outrage. *A Doll's House* challenged established social values at a deep level. Government and church officials spoke out against the play and some theatres in Germany even refused to allow its performance. Ibsen was put under considerable pressure to rewrite his original ending to soften the revolutionary impact of his message. However, in spite of (or perhaps because of) this harsh criticism, the play was translated into many languages and performed all over the world. Ibsen himself became an international figure and the playwright, George Bernard Shaw, even considered him more important than Shakespeare. Today, he is seen as the father of modern drama and many of the most important plays written in the twentieth century, such as Arthur Miller's *Death of a Salesman*, have their roots in Ibsen's idea of the problem play or modern tragedy. The play is also still frequently performed and reinterpreted for modern audiences. Interestingly, modern critics have extended critical readings to explore the role of Torvald, speculating on the fact that he is as trapped by social expectations as Nora. Here, the traditional feminist readings of the play have been extended to encompass a masculinist reading.

This leads us on to your own personal reading of a text which we must not lose sight of within this journey. With an informed awareness of a text's background and some knowledge of other readers' responses, you should be well placed to construct your own reading. If you lose a sense of your own personal response to a text, then this has become merely a sterile intellectual exercise. You might ask yourself the following questions as you construct your reading:

- Have you considered the various different critical schools discussed at the beginning of this chapter? What different readings would these schools produce of Ibsen's play? How convincing do you find these?
- What are your own values and attitudes? How do these help you, as a reader, respond both to the original text and to critical readings you have considered?
- Do you find yourself at odds with or endorsing the text's values and attitudes? Remember, as a critical reader, you are perfectly at liberty to take issue with writers who have long been an established part of our literary canon, such as Shakespeare.
- How successfully does the text use language and genre to convey its ideas?

In particular, with your reading of Ibsen you might consider whether, in our world of equal opportunities, Ibsen's message is too remote to have modern relevance. Or are we still struggling to define the nature of marriage and the roles of men and women even in our contemporary world?

And, finally, remember that no reading is final. You may construct a coherent, well-argued reading today, but may well change your mind tomorrow. Every reading of a text is temporary and forms part of a larger dynamic that is called interpretation.

Exercise 3

We have been examining a literary text, Ibsen's play *A Doll's House*, to illustrate some of the principles that are fundamental for historical criticism. In this exercise, you can begin to apply these principles to a non-literary text.

Look at the following advertisement for Magnet Kitchens which is taken from *Good Housekeeping* magazine in 2002. Carry out a full analysis of this text, focusing on:

- The representation of both class and gender within the advertisement, considering how attitudes and values reflected in this modern text contrast with or perhaps replicate those expressed in Ibsen's earlier text
- The importance of issues of genre, authorship and purpose with the modern text – again you might want to compare this with the Ibsen
- How does the language use reflect its modern context?

Suggestions for answer are at the back of the book.

Figure 1.1 This advertisement for Magnet Kitchens appeared in the September 2002 issue of *Good Housekeeping*

Reproduced by courtesy of Magnet Kitchens

SUMMARY

This chapter has done the following:

- Laid the theoretical foundations to be used in later chapters
- Introduced and defined the notion of historical criticism
- Given examples of how to approach this criticism with both literary and non-literary texts focusing on: attitudes and values, genre, language and reader response

ATTITUDES AND VALUES: THE LEGEND OF KING ARTHUR

CHAPTER 2

The rest of this book gives further opportunities for developing your skills and builds on the foundations laid within the first chapter. The focus is on the skills applicable in reading any text and, while a series of examples will be used which explore particular historical texts, they are intended to demonstrate the techniques appropriate to historical criticism generally.

Many would say that we live in an age where 'history' is valued over 'myth'. History is seen as 'the truth' about the past, a truth that can be approached through an objective and almost scientific study of original documents. Myths, on the other hand, are viewed as no more than fictional stories. However, this distinction has not always existed so clearly. The term 'legend' was originally applied to the lives of the saints and, in an earlier age where greater priority was given to religion, these stories were probably accepted as 'true' by the monks and nuns who knew them. Now, we tend to view these narratives as largely fictional with occasional passages of historical information.

However, the need to create mythologies still exists and can be seen in the press representation of Princess Diana after her death. Why did so many people begin to see Diana as a modern saint? The answer perhaps lies not in our need for historical accuracy but in our need for beliefs and values to shape our lives. Similarly, the myth of King Arthur is usually associated with the image of a medieval court and jousting knights; if there were a historical Arthur, however, he was probably a Celtic chieftain living many years before that time. Other factors have influenced the development of the Arthur legend, factors that are more a reflection of the attitudes and values of later ages.

Postmodernism questions the notion of anyone having unbiased access to the past. It has questioned the very basis of our quest for 'truth' and rather sees that the world consists of a range of ideologies competing with each other for dominance. Central to this is the notion that language governs our view of the world and gives sense and structure to the raw data of experience. Some ideologies may have greater prominence at different times. We live in an age of science, where the values of rational **discourse** and empirical study are given greatest priority. This shapes our approach to history. Earlier societies would have had different values, more probably grounded in religious faith rather than science, and would consequently have given more priority to mythic discourses. Your task as a student of English is to determine what ideas and values are being presented by a text, whether that text is traditionally defined as history, myth or legend.

A good place to start looking at this in greater detail is that shadowy ground that has already been mentioned, one where history, myth and legend have become mixed: the Arthur story.

Exercise 1

Most people will be familiar with at least part of the Arthur legend in one form or another. Note down what you know about the stories: the individual characters, what happens to them and what kind of world we enter when we retell these stories.

Suggestions for Answer

The Arthur Legend

Individual details will vary, but most people have some ideas about the Arthur legend. One of the earliest known versions was written by Geoffrey of Monmouth, a Benedictine monk writing in the twelfth century, several centuries after the historical Arthur probably lived.

Arthur is the son of Uther Pendragon and Igraine and is promised long life, riches and virtue by magical powers. He becomes King of Britain and defeats many enemies with his special sword, Excalibur. He is usually depicted in charge of a medieval court, the legendary Camelot, from which individual knights leave on various adventures and where equality is established through a special arrangement, the Round Table, which avoided giving priority to any leader. Arthur's queen is Guinevere, but the success and honour of Arthur's court are damaged when Guinevere commits adultery with Arthur's best and most valiant knight, Sir Lancelot. The land is thrown into decline as a result of this betrayal, a decline that can only be reversed by finding the Holy Grail (the cup that Christ used at the Last Supper). Eventually, the Grail is found by Sir Galahad, Lancelot's son, and Sir Perceval. Arthur is assisted during his reign by the shadowy figure of Merlin, a wizard or prophet, whose magic assists Arthur. Legend has it that Arthur was born in Tintagel, Cornwall, lived in the castle of Camelot and is buried in Avalon, Glastonbury.

There are many versions of the Arthur story and you may have encountered one of the many twentieth-century representations such as the novel *The Once and Future King* by T. H. White or the films *First Knight* or *Excalibur*. Most people visualise a medieval setting, with knights in armour, jousting tournaments, beautiful ladies and a clear set of moral values that include bravery, nobility and goodness.

IDEALISING THE LEGEND: THE CHIVALRIC CODE

This Arthur, then, who fuels most people's perceptions comes from the medieval period. Most of the stories that are now seen as central to the Arthur myth were gathered together by the French medieval poet Chrétien de Troyes, but the better known work is Sir Thomas Malory's *Le Morte d'Arthur* (first published in 1485). Malory is frequently credited with the creation of the romantic Age of Chivalry. The world he presents is one based on a chivalric code of bravery, skill and honour. Medieval society had a strong sense of hierarchy with levels assigned to the king, dukes, earls, counts, knights and peasants and those lower in this system pledged allegiance to those above them. Women were viewed as remote objects of love and idealised as pure and faithful. The male and female worlds were rigidly separated.

Malory and Arthur in History

Malory was largely responsible for the creation of this Arthur myth which bears little resemblance to an Arthur who may well have been a Celtic chieftain operating even before the invention of armour! More importantly, even Malory's own context is not straightforward as he was writing towards the end of the medieval period when things were starting to change. At that time, the strict hierarchical relations of kings and knights were already being challenged by Renaissance ideas. Power and prestige were gradually becoming available to those with aptitude rather than merely noble birth, a change illustrated by Thomas Wolsey, who had been born the son of a butcher in 1475, and was to rise to become Lord Chancellor, the most powerful commoner in England after the King, by 1515. Malory's work was also among the first to be published on William Caxton's new printing press, itself an opportunity for more people to have access to cheap written works. So, both politically and technologically, the work was essentially at odds with the exclusive, chivalric society that it represented as it emerged from a time when people were beginning to question privilege and status.

Malory's representation of the chivalric code might then be seen as an outdated attempt to preserve an older way of life, one that was already disappearing. Interestingly, perhaps even Malory himself was aware of this tension; in his story, the chivalric ideal is not confidently presented as Arthur is too weak and Lancelot betrays him.

The following exercises will show how the romantic myth, however flawed, has kept its appeal even through further changes in society.

Exercise 2

The Victorian poet, Alfred Lord Tennyson, was fascinated by the world that Malory evoked and wrote his own version, *Idylls of the King*, in 1870. However, much earlier in his career he had already tackled the subject in a poem first written in 1833 called *The Lady of Shalott*.

Read the following text which describes Sir Lancelot and answer the questions:

- How does Tennyson's language here capture a sense of Lancelot? Try to focus on particular groupings of words or semantic fields that describe him
- What does this description of Lancelot tell us about Tennyson's view of the chivalric code?
- How might critics from different schools respond to this, e.g. a feminist or Marxist critic (see chapter 1 to remind yourself of the focus of these different readings)? How would you assess these views?
- What is your own view of this extract?

> A bow-shot from her bower-eaves,
> He rode between the barley-sheaves,
> The sun came dazzling thro' the leaves,
> And flamed upon the brazen greaves[1]
>   Of bold Sir Lancelot.
> A red-cross knight for ever kneel'd
> To a lady in his shield,
> That sparkled on the yellow field,
>   Beside remote Shalott.
>
> The gemmy bridle glitter'd free,
> Like to some branch of stars we see
> Hung in the golden Galaxy.
> The bridle bells rang merrily
>   As he rode down to Camelot;
> And from his blazon'd baldric[2] slung
> A mighty silver bugle hung,
> And as he rode his armour rung,
>   Beside remote Shalott.
>
> All in the blue unclouded weather
> Thick-jewell'd shone the saddle-leather,
> The helmet and the helmet-feather
> Burn'd like one burning flame together,
>   As he rode down to Camelot.
> As often thro' the purple night,

---

1 Armour for the lower leg made of brass
2 A belt or girdle hung diagonally across the body from shoulder to opposite hip decorated with a coat of arms

> Below the starry clusters bright,
> Some bearded meteor, trailing light,
>   Moves over still Shalott.
>
> His broad clear brow in sunlight glow'd;
> On burnish'd hooves his war-horse trode;
> From underneath his helmet flow'd
> His coal-black curls as on he rode,
>   As he rode down to Camelot.
> From the bank and from the river
> He flash'd into the crystal mirror,
> 'Tirra lirra,' by the river
>   Sang Sir Lancelot.

Suggestions for Answer

There are several semantic fields established by Tennyson in this text which give a clear sense of Lancelot and the poet's attitude to the chivalric code. These include:

- Weaponry and armour: bow-shot, greaves, shield, baldric, armour, helmet, helmet-feather
- Horses: rode, bridle, saddle-leather, hooves, war-horse
- Light, sun and stars: sun, dazzling, sparkled, glitter'd, stars, Galaxy, shone, starry clusters bright, bearded meteor, trailing light, sunlight glow'd, flash'd
- Fire: flamed, burn'd, burning flame
- Precious metal and jewels: brazen, gemmy, golden, silver, thick-jewell'd, burnish'd
- Sound: rang merrily, bugle, armour rung, 'tirra lirra', sang
- Colour: red-cross, yellow, golden, blue, purple, coal-black
- Movement: rode (repeated several times), free, moves, trailing, trode, flow'd, flash'd.

Clearly, Tennyson wishes to create a picture of a heroic, handsome knight who makes a significant impact on his environment by his confident riding and singing. He is also described as 'bold' and has a 'broad clear brow'. He is contrasted with the static knight for ever kneeling in his shield and the 'remote Shalott'. Tennyson appears to be presenting a largely stereotypical image of a 'knight in shining armour'.

There are several possible responses to this text. A feminist critic may highlight the linking of action, movement and fiery imagery with the male world and contrast this in particular with the static, imprisoned Lady who appears in the rest of the poem. A Marxist critic may highlight the strict hierarchical society that is represented here and the obvious wealth that Lancelot exudes centred on the romantic depiction of the countryside. The absence of poor people in the poem may be problematical for a Marxist critic, especially in view of the fact that Tennyson was writing at a time when urban poverty in Victorian towns was a significant social problem. On the other hand, you may well have enjoyed the richly evocative language that Tennyson uses and, from an aesthetic viewpoint (i.e. one concerned only with the poem as a work of art), valued the poem on that level.

Tennyson and History

Although Tennyson based his work on Malory, he was writing at a very different time with very different values and attitudes. Victorian interest in the medieval period stems from the work of Walter Scott (1771–1832) who depicted knights, ladies and jousting tournaments in his novels and poetry. In fact, there were many real jousting tournaments staged at this time and these are frequently represented in the novels of the day such as Disraeli's *Coningsby* (1844) and Trollope's *Barchester Towers* (1857), the latter mocking the practice. There was also an interest in medieval architecture (called Gothic) and a desire to return to a society where chivalry was viewed as an ideal of masculine conduct supported by a caring and charitable Catholic religion with monks and nuns dispensing both spiritual and physical salvation. In art, this influence could be seen in the paintings of the Pre-Raphaelite Brotherhood who also painted images from Tennyson's poems.

Inevitably, this obsession with the past says something very significant about Victorian society itself. The Industrial Revolution had started to create a society of increasing urbanisation as the old methods of working the land gave way to factories and the rise of new wealth. This society was seen, by many, as increasingly ugly, materialistic and selfish. Traditional aristocratic values were being challenged by a new rising class of industrialists no longer interested in old courtly codes of behaviour. Some artists sought to escape what they saw as the ugliness of this new world by retreating to an older world of positive values.

Extension ideas

In one sense, then, Tennyson was challenging the dominant ideology of his own time and, in common with other artists of the day, returning to an earlier historical period, which was completely idealised, to do this. However, how far has Tennyson simply accepted the chivalric code? You will need to read the whole poem to answer this question fully, but you might start to consider how far Lancelot is presented as an ideal. With whom do our sympathies lie in the whole poem? If the chivalric code presented women as unobtainable ideals, what is the effect of this? How far do you think Tennyson is aware of this conflict?

Remember that while we try to establish general patterns to allow us to create readings, the individual writer will always have their own perspective on these issues and the process of untangling this is full of ambiguities and uncertainties.

The Kennedys and Camelot

The next example illustrates the process of history becoming myth in action. On 20 January 1961, John F. Kennedy was sworn in as the thirty-fifth President of the United States and his short term of office was to create a new American myth. Lines from Kennedy's inaugural speech – 'Ask not what your country can do for you, ask what you can do for your country' – are still remembered and the President's official home, the White House, became a place to celebrate American achievement. Jackie, Kennedy's wife, carefully restored all its rooms with the finest art and furniture and the Kennedy administration came to represent glamour, style, good looks, wealth, compassion and family life. In addition, Kennedy was the youngest ever President and the first Roman Catholic. In June 1963, Kennedy's Civil Rights bill sought to end the racism at the heart of American society, particularly in the southern states. The adulation of Kennedy reached even greater heights when the President was assassinated in November 1963.

Shortly after this assassination, Kennedy's wife, Jackie, gave an interview to the American *Life* magazine about what had happened. The journalist was Theodore White and his notes from this interview became available in 1995, one year after Jackie Kennedy's death, creating renewed interest in the original. The following extract is taken from an ABC News article about the interview:

In the exclusive interview, Jackie recounted for the first and last time the events of the assassination in Dallas, providing graphic details of the shooting and vivid descriptions of the drive. In the margins of his notepad, White noted 'her calm voice and total recall' of the events.

Then she confessed, 'I'm so ashamed of myself – all I keep thinking of is this line from a musical comedy.'

Camelot, the Broadway musical starring Richard Burton and Julie Andrews, had opened in December 1960, a few weeks after Kennedy was elected president. The Kennedys had attended the show and loved it.

Jackie told White that at night, they would listen to a recording of the musical on their Victrola before they went to sleep. Jack's favorite song came at the very end of the musical and his favorite lines were, 'Don't let it be forgot, that once there was a spot, for one brief shining moment that was known as Camelot.'

'There'll be great presidents again – and the Johnsons are wonderful, they've been wonderful to me – but there'll never be another Camelot again,' she said. White's notes, now known as the *Camelot Papers*, suggest that this was anything but an off-hand reference: 'all she could repeat was, "Tell people there will never be that Camelot again".'

Exercise 3

This article implies that Jackie Kennedy's use of the Arthur myth was far from coincidental. What do you think she was suggesting by the reference?

Suggestions for Answer

The ABC News article gives the impression that this interview was a very clever piece of **propaganda**. Jackie Kennedy has used an **intertextual** reference to the 1960 Broadway musical, one that would appeal to a large number of her readers. In particular, she is implicitly referring to the romantic chivalric code. Kennedy is presented as a 'man of the people' through the story of his love for this show and his replaying of the record. The mention of the 'Victrola' shows that he was very much a man of his time, using the latest technologies (here, a record player). Even the timing is cited as significant: Kennedy was elected president a few weeks after the opening of the show and so the two leaders, one historical and one mythological, are fundamentally linked.

The quotation from the musical endorses this idealisation of John F. Kennedy (interestingly, this was quoted incorrectly at first and was corrected for the written interview – a good example of the differences between speech and writing). The adjective 'shining' relates back to Tennyson's semantic field of stars, but here it is further modified by 'brief'. The phrase 'there'll never be' is repeated to emphasise the uniqueness of the Kennedy years and the proper noun 'Camelot' links Kennedy's White House with the legendary castle. Jackie Kennedy uses the legend as a way of perpetuating Kennedy's image and conveying him as a noble, heroic, honourable and chivalric leader fundamentally in touch with the needs and values of his people.

Jackie Kennedy and History

Since Kennedy's death, more and more details have emerged about the Kennedys and it is clear that their marriage was not the fairy-tale romance that this interview implies. The couple actually spent little time together and Kennedy came to be notorious for affairs with other women. However, Jackie wanted Americans to remember her husband in a special way far removed from the sex scandals and cynicism that could so easily have dogged his reputation. During his time in the White House, there were serious confrontations with the communist Soviet Union over both Berlin and Cuba, so, politically, the Camelot **allusion** retrospectively endorsed the USA as a land of nobility and democracy. Camelot being the home of the Round Table, there is an implication of equality (between knights, at least!) which is an easy contrast with conventional representations of the Soviet Union at that time as a repressive regime where personal freedom was restricted. It is interesting that this allusion continues to be used and a recent book on the Kennedy family, *The Dynasty* by Hugh Sidey, talks about the 'children of Camelot'.

Exercise 4

Read the following internet page that gives background information about a flour company in Vermont, USA. Discuss the language and presentation of this page, exploring in particular the way this company has used the Arthur legend for its own purposes.

Suggestions for answer are not provided for this exercise.

Home ● Recipes ● **Our Company** ● Baking Center
Flour for Home Bakers ● Flour for Professional Bakers
Sharpen Your Baking Skills ● Shop Online ● In the News

The King Arthur Flour Company: Past, Present, and Future
Where the Round Table is made real...

- Our history
- Company profile
- Employment

In 1896, The King Arthur Flour Company's three owners were stumped.

Mark Taylor, George Wood, and Orin Sands were rolling out a new flour, but they were stumped on the name. They needed to somehow express the flour's premium characteristics -- its integrity, strength, reliability, and superior performance. As you know by now, they chose the name King Arthur, a name so powerful it eventually stood for the company itself.

Today, we are over 160 owners. And we realize that being named after the legendary knight carries the obligation of upholding his virtues. This obligation reaches through our products to our very business dealings. Like our predecessors of 1896, we want our products and corporate life to express the same integrity, strength, reliability, and superior performance.

That's why, when stumped for a new management approach in the early 1990's, we again looked to the Arthurian round table for inspiration. It seemed only natural to structure ourselves the way Arthur and his knights did, as a team built on inclusion and collaboration. In 1996, we launched an Employee Stock Ownership Plan (ESOP), putting ownership of The King Arthur Flour Company in the hands of everyone at the table.

The result is a corporate culture of incredible passion and sincerity that propels us to honor our customers and celebrate a company we can truly call our own. Some may scoff at such high ideals in today's business world. But to us, there is no other way to successfully run a company -- especially your own.

Contact Us ● Home ● **Top of Page** ● Join The Baking Circle(sm)

Figure 2.1 The 2003 website of a US firm, the King Arthur Flour Company, which draws on the legend of Arthur 'the once and future king'

Reproduced by courtesy of the King Arthur Flour Company

CHALLENGING THE LEGEND

In the first part of this chapter, we have looked at the use that writers at different times have made of the idealising potential of the Arthur myth. However, we have also considered the fact that, even though these writers have frequently been interpreted as promoting the chivalric ideal, the reality even here is often more sophisticated. The importance of exploring the individual text with an awareness of contextual issues but without preconceived ideas is an important part of your act of interpretation.

We now turn to some more explicitly cynical uses of the legend. The first is an extract from Mark Twain's *A Connecticut Yankee in King Arthur's Court* published in 1889 in the USA. The novel centres on the adventures of Hank Morgan. Hank suffers a blow to the head which renders him unconscious; when he awakes, he is in Camelot in the year 528. The novel is narrated in first person from his perspective.

Exercise 5

In the following text, the narrator approaches a strange castle. What attitudes and values are reflected here that contrast with the romantic chivalric ideal we have seen earlier?

If knights errant were to be believed, not all castles were desirable places to seek hospitality in. As a matter of fact, knights errant were *not* persons to be believed – that is, measured by modern standards of veracity; yet, measured by the standards of their own time, and scaled accordingly, you got the truth. It was very simple: you discounted a statement ninety-seven per-cent; the rest was fact. Now after making this allowance, the truth remained that if I could find out something about the castle before ringing the door-bell – I mean hailing the warders – it was the sensible thing to do. So I was pleased when I saw in the distance a horseman making the bottom turn of the road that wound down from this castle.

As we approached each other, I saw that he wore a plumed helmet and seemed to be otherwise clothed in steel, but bore a curious addition also – a stiff square garment like a herald's tabard. However, I had to smile at my own forgetfulness when I got nearer and read this sign on his tabard:

'Persimmons's Soap – All the Prime-Donne Use It.'

That was a little idea of my own, and had several wholesome purposes in view toward the civilizing and uplifting of this nation.

Suggestions for Answer

Twain both challenges the chivalric ideal, here, and sets up some very different values for our approval, primarily through the use of humour. On the one hand, he questions one of the central aspects of the chivalric code – truthfulness – by his initial joke about the fact that knights cannot be trusted. This implies that the tales of valour and bravery told by knights are mainly fabrication. We then see a real knight who is described in a very similar way to Lancelot in Tennyson's poem with a 'plumed helmet' and 'clothed in steel'. However, this visual image is then mocked by the fact that the knight is wearing an advertisement for soap, something that the narrator himself takes credit for as a 'little idea'. This not only is **anachronistic** (out of time) but also trivialises what the knight stands for. The narrator clearly values cleanliness (in the use of soap) more than he does valour. He is also using the knight to advertise a product: advertising is the basis of a commercial, materialistic society very much at odds with chivalric society. The narrator also clearly values prudence and caution above bravery and risk. Where the knights would storm an unknown castle without hesitation, the narrator waits to find out more information before he knocks. Again, humour is created by his anachronistic reference to 'ringing the door-bell'.

Twain and History

Twain's novel generated great controversy when it was published and, particularly in England, his use of the Arthurian legend was seen as irreverent and inappropriate. Twain had already included a scene in his earlier novel *Huckleberry Finn* (1884) where a wrecked steamboat is discovered to be called the *Walter Scott*. Twain believed that Walter Scott's representations of medieval life had had a negative effect on art and literature because Scott idealised what Twain interpreted as a society based on inherited power, lack of freedom and a corrupt Catholic Church. Twain saw himself as both a realist and a democrat, and he tried to debunk the Arthur myth as the Victorians perceived it. He deplored the aristocratic pretensions of parts of America at that time, believing that these reflected the negative influence of England, although he had no objection to making money through new industry. His view of society is based on values of common sense, prudence, cleanliness and modern conveniences.

Twain also uses this novel to explore other political and social issues that relate more to his own society than any other. Later in the novel, the narrator encounters a group of slaves, one of whom is cruelly whipped. The narrator says:

> I wanted to stop the whole thing and set the slaves free, but that would not do. I must not interfere too much and get myself a name for riding over the country's laws and the citizens' rights roughshod. If I lived and prospered

continued

I would be the death of slavery, that I was resolved upon; but I would try to fix it so that when I became its executioner it should be by command of the nation.

Historically, medieval society did not have a system of slavery (although feudalism did dictate everyone's status within a clearly marked hierarchy). However, if you research Twain's own context and, in particular, some of the ideas he explores in *Huckleberry Finn*, you will see that this passage relates far more to Twain's own attitudes and values than to anything medieval. *Huckleberry Finn* shows a society where many people accept unquestioningly the right to own other people as a possession and the novel is an extended critique of this. Twain clearly returns to this in his later novel. So, yet again, a writer's context and their engagement with contemporary issues become the most pressing concern in their work.

Exercise 6

The following extract is taken from the screenplay of the film *Monty Python and the Holy Grail*, a comedy, which was first released in 1974. King Arthur and his knights have just arrived at Camelot.

- What impression are we given here of the authors' attitudes and values?
- How is the Arthur legend used in this text?
- What is significant about the choice of genre here?

Suggestions for answer are at the back of the book.

LANCELOT	[*he points*]: Look, my Liege.
	[*They all stop and look.*]
ARTHUR	[*with thankful reverence*]: Camelot!
	[*Cut to shot of amazing castle in the distance. Illuminated in the rays of the setting sun.* *Music.* *Cut back to* ARTHUR *and the group. They are all staring with fascination.*]
GALAHAD:	Camelot . . .
LANCELOT:	Camelot . . .
GAWAIN	[*at the back, to* PAGE]: It's only a model.
ARTHUR	[*turning sharply*]: Sh! [*To the rest.*] Knights! I bid you welcome to your new home! Let us ride . . . to Camelot!

[*Cut to interior of medieval hall. A large group of armoured* KNIGHTS *are engaged in a well-choreographed song-and-dance routine of the very up-beat 'If they could see me now' type of fast bouncy number. The poorer verses are made clearer by cutting to a group of* KNIGHTS *actually engaged in the described task while the line itself is sung. They sing:*]

KNIGHTS: We're Knights of the Round Table
   We dance whene'er we're able
   We do routines and chorus scenes
   With footwork impeccable
   We dine well here in Camelot
   We eat ham and jam and Spam a lot.

   We're Knights of the Round Table
   Our shows are formidable
   But many times
   We're given rhymes
   That are quite unsingable
   We're opera mad in Camelot
   We sing from the diaphragm a lot.

[*Booming basses. A routine where two* XYLOPHONISTS *play parts of* KNIGHTS' *armour producing a pleasing effect.*]

KNIGHTS: In war we're tough and able,
   Quite indefatigable
   Between our quests
   We sequin vests
   And impersonate Clark Gable
   It's a busy life in Camelot.
SINGLE MAN: I have to push the pram a lot.

[*Cut back to* ARTHUR *and* BEDEVERE *and* COMPANY *as we had left them.*]

ARTHUR: No, on second thoughts let's not go to Camelot.
KNIGHTS: Right!
ARTHUR: It is a silly place.

Exercise 7 – Producing Your Own Writing

Choose part of the Arthur story and rewrite it within a contemporary context. You may want to approach the story from any of the schools of criticism that we discussed in chapter 1 – feminist, Marxist, post-colonial, queer theory – and think about how modern concerns should be addressed in your transformation. You will also want to consider which genre is most appropriate for your work. Then, write a commentary reflecting on how you have used the story to convey your own values and attitudes.

SUMMARY

This chapter has done the following:

- Used the theoretical approach established in chapter 1 across a range of texts to illustrate the principles being discussed
- Defined the notion of ideology and illustrated this through textual analysis
- Explored concepts such as myth, history and legend in greater detail

---

ATTITUDES AND VALUES: HISTORY AND REGIONAL IDENTITY

CHAPTER 3

So far, we have explored texts that represent different facets of the King Arthur legend and have used this to illustrate certain aspects of the dynamic relationship that exists between a text and its context. The King Arthur stories are a useful way of illustrating the way different ideologies can be conveyed in language at different times by different societies.

In this chapter, we will examine this process more closely by considering a range of texts that convey a sense of regional **identity**. Identity itself is a concept of central importance for critics working within fields such as Marxism, feminism and post-colonialism (see chapter 1) where issues such as class, gender and race provide a major focus for interpretation. These critics would argue that our personal identity is created from a range of individual (psychological, biographical) and collective (social, historical) factors and they examine how these are represented in both literary and non-literary texts. They claim that the way in which people from, for example, a range of different classes are presented in a text gives us crucial information about the attitudes of the author (and, perhaps, in broader terms some aspects of that author's society). This often also highlights issues of *power* because certain groups of people are given characteristics that are seen as in some way more valuable or dominant than others. These are called representations because they are an attempt by writers to re-create 'reality' and to place meaning on very complex and variable material. Looking at texts from this perspective can provide a particularly fruitful way of exploring and comparing attitudes and values.

The following exercise will illustrate this process.

SCOTTISH HISTORY AND WILLIAM WALLACE

Scottish attempts to resist assimilation into a United Kingdom under the dominance of England have flavoured both Scottish political and literary life since medieval times. This exercise examines a key historical figure – William Wallace – who has often been used as a symbol of Scottish identity. We will explore the way he has been interpreted at different times by different authors.

As has already been illustrated with the Arthur legend, it is impossible to access a set of 'facts' that summarise William Wallace's place in history without some kind of bias from the writer. The following summary gives you some information about Wallace's place in Scottish history but is, as everything else produced by language, yet another version.

During the thirteenth century, Edward I, king of England, carried out several military campaigns seeking to extend his territories in Scotland, Wales and France. At this time, Scotland was ruled by its own king with complete political independence. By the end of this century, however, Edward had largely established his supremacy over Scotland, although he retained power by a ruthless policy designed to eliminate any opposition. In 1297, the cruelty of the English led to the rising of William Wallace, a lowborn Scottish leader, who initially led a resistance with great success. However, by 1305, Wallace had been captured and executed, although the Scots continued to resist English dominance successfully under Robert the Bruce.

Exercise 1

Read the following two extracts which both deal with the death of William Wallace. Text A is taken from *Notes on British History* by William Edwards, MA and was published in 1953; Text B is taken from *Braveheart* by Randall Wallace and was published in 1995.

Comment on the way Wallace's death is represented in these texts, considering:

- How the use of language reflects the authors' attitudes and values
- Ways in which you think these authors' own contexts may be reflected in their personal reading and interpretations of William Wallace

Text A

The second conquest of Scotland 1304.

Stirling captured and Wallace executed, 1305. Edward's nephew, the Earl of Richmond, made governor. Justices and sheriffs appointed, Celtic laws abolished. The Scottish Parliament kept. The claim of Boniface VIII to suzerainty[1] over Scotland denied.

An excellent scheme, but their love of independence prevented the Scots from accepting the supremacy of a foreign king.

---

1 Supremacy

Text B

The disembowelment began. The magistrate leaned in beside Wallace's ear. 'It can all end. Right now! Bliss. Peace. Just say it. Cry out. *Mercy!* Yes? . . . Yes?'

The crowd could not hear the magistrate, but they knew the procedure and they, too, goaded Wallace, chanting, 'Mer-cy! Mer-cy!'

Wallace's eyes rolled to the magistrate, who signaled for quiet and shouted, 'The prisoner wishes to say a word!'

There was silence.

Hamish and Stephen were weeping as each in his own way prayed: 'Mercy, William . . . Say "mercy". . . '

Wallace's eyes fluttered and cleared. He fought through the pain, struggled for one last deep breath, and screamed, '*FREEEE-DOMMMMMM!*'

Suggestions for Answer

Text A is written in a style that immediately conveys a sense of objective historical accuracy. This is created by the elevated and legalistic lexis ('suzerainty', 'Celtic laws') and a distinctive style of syntax. The book's title – _Notes on British History_ – dictates this style with short, occasionally incomplete (or minor) sentences used throughout, often created by the omission of complete verbs ('Stirling captured'), to give an impression that the text is a concise and unemotive summary of factual information, not opinion. Adjectives are kept to a minimum and factual information is given, such as dates and places. The author's intellectual credentials are emphasised by the inclusion of his qualifications after his name (MA). Wallace's execution is conveyed in a small number of words without comment.

However, on closer examination, it becomes clear that this is not simply an unbiased account giving the reader a doorway to the 'truth'. The writer comments that the placing of Edward's nephew as governor in place of the local Scottish king is an 'excellent scheme' (a rare use of an adjective) and the legal lexis used to explain the arrangements ('justices', 'sheriffs', 'Celtic laws', 'parliament') implies a reliable and specialised form of government. This is unacceptable to the Scots because of 'their love of independence', the pronoun 'their' implying distance and a readership that is not Scottish. The implication also appears to be that the irrational and perhaps childlike Scots protested against a perfectly acceptable legal arrangement simply because of their idealistic notions about 'freedom'. The text was written for an English schools audience in 1953 at a time when, although many colonial countries were gaining their freedom from English dominance (e.g. India in 1947), Scottish independence would not have been viewed as a serious political option.

Text B in many ways endorses the image of the Scots created in the first extract and yet for a very different purpose and audience. This is a fictional dramatisation of Wallace's death, told in third person **narrative voice**, aimed at creating maximum emotional impact. Because this is the 'book of the film' it is likely that most readers would have seen the film and therefore have a clear visual image of the events and the actors. The reader, and indeed the viewer of the film, is positioned, not as an outsider as with Text A, but as an insider watching and sympathising with Wallace's sacrifice. The extract is mainly delivered in dialogue, reflecting its relation to the film script, and sentences to progress the narrative are often simple using the simple past tense to create maximum impact ('There was silence'). Suspense is consciously created by the build-up to Wallace's death and his final word is deeply significant: 'freedom' (expressed in capitals with repeated letters to replicate Wallace's defiant shout) and has important **connotations** for a modern western reader. By choosing a novel or film script, the author can create Wallace as a character, one with whom a reader or audience can have sympathy and his death becomes thus emotionally charged.

The author of this text is American, but he signals his relationship with the historical Wallace via his own name (Randall Wallace). During the 1990s, the issue of Scottish devolution from England became an important political issue and by 1998 the Scotland Act had been passed which devolved significant political power to a new Scottish Parliament. However, what is interesting is how popular this film (and the rather idealised notion of Scottish independence) became in the USA. Perhaps many Americans saw this story as part of their own heritage and, like Randall Wallace who cites a trip to Edinburgh as the inspiration for the book, had a romantic belief in their own Celtic roots? Perhaps they drew parallels between Wallace's stand for freedom and their own challenge to English supremacy in the American War of Independence?

Overall, though, both texts, in very different ways, can be seen to raise issues of power and identity focusing on the relationship between Scotland and England (and, by implication, the USA in Text B).

ACCENT AND DIALECT

Identity, particularly regional identity, can be conveyed in many ways and Scotland has worked hard to retain its individual cultural identity in its traditions, its own legal and educational system and, in particular, through its language. Before 1603, Scotland was a kingdom with its own ruler, a separate political unit (although, as we have seen, this was often fiercely contested); however, in 1603 James VI of Scotland also became James I of England, effectively joining the two thrones. In 1707, the two Parliaments joined and Scotland was joined with England via an Act of Union. Thus, it became even more important for the Scottish to keep a sense of cultural distinctness and the Scottish language became a key focus for this. On the one hand, Scotland's own language – Gaelic – has survived, a language with a linguistic development completely different from that of English; on the other hand, Scotland has developed its own distinctive version of English known as Scots.

Regional talk is an important way in our society for speakers to retain a sense of individuality. An accent reflects a particular pronunciation of words linked to a regional area whereas a dialect reflects choice of words and grammatical structures. There is a range of regional accents and dialects across the British Isles, and these different ways of speaking are valued in different ways. **Received pronunciation** and **Standard English** are the accent and dialect with the most prestige and are most commonly encountered in government, the law and the education system. (See also Amanda Coultas's *Language and Social Contexts* in this series.)

The next two exercises will allow you to look at this area in greater depth by considering texts by Scottish authors from different historical periods for whom accent and dialect are central concerns.

Exercise 2

The following extract is taken from James Hogg's *The Private Memoirs and Confessions of a Justified Sinner*, first published in 1824. Hogg was born in 1770 in Scotland to a family of impoverished farmers and worked for many years as a cow-herd. Even after he became famous, he continued to supplement his income through farming and became known as the Ettrick Shepherd (referring to the parish in Scotland where he was born and his farming roots). The following episode from his most famous work depicts a court scene about a third of the way into the book.

- Explore the way Hogg represents accent and dialect in this extract to establish issues of power and identity. Consider in particular how the **setting** of the text contributes to this.

The maid was first called; and when she came into the witnesses' box, the anxious and hopeless looks of the prisoner were manifest to all: But the girl, whose name, she said, was Bessy Gillies, answered in so flippant and fearless a way, that the audience were much amused. After a number of routine questions, the depute-advocate asked her if she was at home on the morning of the fifth of September last, when her mistress' house was robbed?

'Was I at hame, say ye? Na, faith-ye, lad! An I had been at hame, there had been mair to dee. I wad hae raised sic a yelloch!'

'Where were you that morning?'

'Where was I, say you? I was in the house where my mistress was, sitting dozing an' half sleeping in the kitchen. I thought aye she would be setting out every minute, for twa hours.'

---

continued

'And when you sent home, what did you find?'

'What found we? Be my sooth, we found a broken lock, an' toom kists.'

'Relate some of the particulars, if you please.'

'O, sir, the thieves didna stand upon particulars: they were hale-sale dealers in a' our best wares.'

'I mean, what passed between your mistress and you on the occasion?'

'What passed, say ye? O, there wasna muckle: I was in a great passion, but she was dung doitrified a wee. When she gaed to put the key i' the door, up it flew to the fer wa'. – "Bess, ye jaud, what's the meaning o' this?" quo she. "Ye hae left the door open, ye tawpie!" quo she.

"The ne'er o' that I did," quo I, "or may my shakel bane never turn another key."'

Scottish dialect words: yelloch = yell; twa = two; toom = empty; kists = chests; didna = did not; hale-sale = wholesale; muckle = much; dung = struck; doitrified = stupefied; gaed = went; fer wa' = far wall; jaud = worthless woman; tawpie = foolish young woman; shakel bane = wrist.

Suggestions for Answer

This extract presents two aspects of power and language. Firstly, the scene presents a court-room where the reader expects to encounter the language of legal power through the figure of the lawyer who is conducting the examination. Secondly, and closely linked to this first point, is the issue of accent and dialect as we can see both Standard English and Scots English used in the dialogue and the narrative. The Scots English is conveyed by **phonetic** spelling where conventional letters are used in an attempt to re-create how the speaker would sound (a more accurate but specialised way of capturing this would be through phonetic transcription which would then no longer be comprehensible for the majority of readers).

The character of Bessy Gillies is introduced to the reader through the third person narrator's comments and she is described as 'flippant and fearless'. She is introduced using the simple noun 'maid' which contrasts with the complex compound noun with its legal flavour, 'depute-advocate', used to describe the lawyer. Legal language is often noted for its complexity and **jargon**, a way of maintaining power for those within its power frame by using specialised words. However, in this extract we see exactly the opposite. Although the **direct speech** is **unattributed**, i.e. the speaker is not made clear through 'he said' and 'she said', the use of both Standard English and dialect makes it obvious who is speaking and identities are established. The lawyer's Standard English is concise, formal and polite with clear **interrogatives** requesting Bessy to tell the court-room what she knows. However, almost every question from the lawyer is followed by a rephrased question from Bessy, almost serving as a translation into her own dialect. She then goes on to answer the question using broad Scottish dialect, overturning the dominance of Standard English by giving the lawyer (and reader) the task of finding the meaning of her words. In addition, although Bessy uses the **address term** 'sir' at one point, she also calls the lawyer by the colloquial term 'lad'. In total, Bessy speaks much more than the lawyer and refuses to summarise or focus her words, insisting on conveying her knowledge in the language and style that suits her best. Conventional power relations in the court are completely subverted and Hogg uses Scots dialect to redirect power from the male, middle-class, Standard-English-using lawyer to the female, working-class, Scots-dialect-using servant.

Hogg and History

Although Hogg was writing over one hundred years after the Union of England and Scotland, he chooses to set his novel at this period, a time when Scottish national identity was in crisis. However, his exploration reveals that this crisis was still current in 1824, Hogg's own context. As mentioned earlier, Hogg was the son of a farmer and tried to make a living from writing poetry and fiction. He moved to Edinburgh in 1810 and found himself in a world where English was considered the language of gentility and Scots was viewed as vulgar and coarse. Those who used the Scots dialect (such as the Scottish poet Robbie Burns – see, for example, *Holy Willie's Prayer*) were considered charmingly rustic and unlearned. This scene from Hogg's novel could be read as a direct challenge to this stereotype and a rejection of English power, both political and linguistic. It is no surprise that contemporary reviews of Hogg's book cite 'the iniquity of bad English' and 'bad grammar' as among the work's most glaring faults. Before the twentieth-century academic discipline of Linguistics developed, accents and dialects were viewed simply as 'bad grammar', diverging from the rules of Standard English.

THE TWENTIETH CENTURY: DEVELOPING ATTITUDES

The eighteenth and nineteenth centuries witnessed the development of literary texts that included characters who spoke with regional accents and dialects yet, in spite of this popularity, by 1872 the Scottish Education Act had banned Scots from schools. Perhaps, in a sense, this action was necessary *because* of this popularity as Scots became associated with a rural and backward-looking form of poetry rather than the language of the educated. The tension between Standard English, with its power base in the south of England and its connections with government and education, and local Scots dialect became more pressing and remained a fundamental aspect of Scotland's sense of identity.

By the twentieth century, literature again saw the revival of Scots and it began to be used increasingly for works deemed to be of serious literary merit; dialect poetry was used for intellectual exploration rather than being seen as quaint and rural. The Scottish poet Hugh MacDiarmid led this revival and by the late twentieth century, an increasing number of writers began to write routinely using dialect. Liz Lochhead is one of the best known of contemporary Scottish writers and her plays have explored many facets of what the *Guardian* has described as 'the myriad sexual, political and religious deformities that still plague the Scottish psyche'. Liz Lochhead as a writer is acutely aware of the tensions that reside in language and has commented that the very word 'dialect' implies there is a right and a wrong way to speak. She prefers the term 'hometown English' which emphasises the importance of our own regional identity. In 1989, Lochhead's play *Mary Queen of Scots Got Her Head Chopped Off* was first published having been performed at the Edinburgh Festival in 1987. The troubled reign of Mary Stuart, Queen of Scotland, has provided inspiration for many writers, and is particularly interesting for its symbolism of the conflict between England and Scotland. Briefly, the historical facts that the play is based on can be summarised as follows:

Elizabeth I's rule over England, from 1558 to 1603, was often characterised by anxiety over those who might have claims to her throne. Mary Stuart was one such claimant through her mother who was Henry VIII's sister, in spite of the fact that Henry had specifically excluded her from the succession in his will. Many also saw Mary's Catholicism as an opportunity for returning England to the 'true religion'. Many conflicts ensued, variously involving Mary's husbands including James Hepburn, Earl of Bothwell, but finally resulting in Mary's imprisonment for many years under Elizabeth's orders. Mary was forced to give up her crown and was finally implicated in the Babington plot, a Catholic conspiracy to assassinate Elizabeth. This resulted in her execution.

Exercise 3

The following text is taken from a scene towards the end of Lochhead's play *Mary Queen of Scots Got Her Head Chopped Off*. Read the extract and then answer the following questions.

- How does Lochhead use language in this extract to reflect power relations?
- What contrasts are set up in this scene?
- Comment on the way Lochhead's use of genre (drama) governs the presentation of her ideas.

Suggestions for answer are at the back of the book.

ELIZABETH: They split her from her Bothwell, drive him from their shores, they seize her infant son, strip her of her crown, lock her in a castle in the middle of an island and throw away the key. And still she can charm some man into helping her escape. God help me, why does she come to England when she could have sailed to bloody France!

[And MARY, all alone, is lit up on the other side of the stage. She holds out her empty arms around an imaginary BOTHWELL and spins in a bitter parody of that dance together ta-ra-ing the same mad waltz tune, then stops still.]

MARY: I said: 'To hell in a white petticoat wi' you Bothwell, oh aye I will go, I maun go.' Wis it love? No, no' whit you thocht, Jamie Hepburn, oh aye, ye were richt I did . . . aye did . . . lust for ye. Wis that whit it wis? At the time I wis ower innocent to ken whit wis steering me. But I ken noo, Bothwell, I ken noo. Dinna think it wis lichtsomely or in love that I lay me doon wi' ye, in the daurk. Naw, it wis despair. Oh and wi' a kinna black joy I reachit oot for you to cover me and smother me and for yin moment, snuff oot the hale birlin' world in stillness. And ilka dawn I woke up wi' ye, I saw disaster a' mapped oot for me, clear as my Davy's magic cairds. The ruined tower, the hangin' man, the Empress on her throne, Judgement . . . and a' thing smashed and skailt for ever tymmelin' a' aroon.

[She sinks down on her knees caught in her tight spot and at the other side of the stage, balancing her, is ELIZABETH in (quite literally) her tight spot. All alone too . . . but for those men and their paper and their pen.]

ELIZABETH: My subjects love me! I am the Virgin Queen! I love my good cousin Queen Mary and will keep her my honoured guest in all luxury in the lavish hospitality of my proudest castle. For her own safety.

And my so-called 'wise advisers' would have to trick me before I would consent to sign a warrant for her death.

Would have to trick me. Trick me. Trick me.

Exercise 4

Text A is taken from a song called 'Heart of the Highland' released by the Scottish band Capercaillie in 1991; Text B is a **sonnet** taken from *Glasgow Sonnets* by Edwin Morgan in 1990.

- Compare the way Scotland is represented in these texts, taking account of language, structure and form as part of your analysis. You should also consider the production context of each work and address how this may have affected their final form.

Suggestions for answer are not provided for this exercise.

Text A

Let the dance begin
Lock away the fine china
And kick up the old stone floor
Where the train divides
Upon Lomondside
Hear the echo from forest to shore
Sailing over deep water
And dancing on air
If you close your eyes
You will be there

Do you dream of a journey
Taking you back to your home
Where the cry from
The heart of the Highland lives on.

Text B

A mean wind wanders through the backcourt trash.
Hackles on puddles rise, old mattresses
puff briefly and subside. Play-fortresses
of brick and bric-a-brac spill out some ash.
Four storeys have no windows left to smash,
but in the fifth a chipped sill buttresses
mother and daughter the last mistresses
of that black block condemned to stand, not crash.
Around them the cracks deepen, the rats crawl.
The kettle whimpers on a crazy hob.
Roses of mould grow from ceiling to wall,
The man lies late since he has lost his job,
smokes on one elbow, letting his coughs fall
thinly into an air too poor to rob.

SUMMARY

This chapter has done the following:

- Extended the theoretical discussion to consider regional identity and its representation over time
- Applied this to a range of texts
- Looked in more detail at accent and dialect and the importance this has for issues of identity

ATTITUDES AND VALUES: HISTORY AND RACE

In the last chapter, we looked at the idea of identity, particularly in relation to the notion of Scottishness. This allowed us both to explore the centrality of language when representing identity (in relation to accent/dialect) and to consider some of the effects of changes over time.

This brings us to extend our consideration of identity to an area that in many ways reflects the concerns of Scottish writers but takes us further afield, an area that is the preserve of post-colonial criticism (see chapter 1). Post-colonial critics focus on countries that were formerly colonised states, mainly in Asia and Africa, those no longer directly administered from the coloniser's seat of power, whether that be London, Paris or another western capital. Although critics had been long aware of imperial themes in literary texts, what these new critics explored was the way that power is created by language and they sought to analyse these discourses (through a process called discourse analysis). If language is central for the creation of identity, then the way colonised countries are represented in western texts is an essential part of this. Just as we have seen with texts focused on Scottishness, colonial texts are even more likely to represent power relations by showing the inferiority of the colonised against the natural superiority of the coloniser.

India provides a fruitful illustration of this process and also gives an opportunity to explore texts from different time periods to see how representations of India have changed and evolved. The process of colonisation was much more gradual in India than, say, Africa. England's relationship with India began as trading partners and European interest in India can be traced back to classical times when Rome traded extensively with India for spices, textiles and other oriental products. Trade continued through the Middle Ages, though trade routes were frequently threatened by competitors such as the Turks or the Mongols. By the fifteenth century, attempts were made to secure trading agreements with India, initially by Portugal and, in 1595, the Dutch sent a first fleet to India to extend their commercial enterprises. The English decided to join this venture and, on the last day of 1600, they formed the East India Company. Initially meeting considerable resistance from other European powers, the British East India Company gradually established itself as the major commercial power in India.

Exercise 1

The following text is taken from Shakespeare's play *A Midsummer Night's Dream* which was probably first published around 1598/9. This section of the play centres on the conflict in the fairy world caused by the decision of Titania, the Fairy Queen, not to allow her husband, Oberon, to take an Indian prince from her because she promised the child's dead mother that she would protect him. The lines are spoken by Titania.

- What impression do you receive from this text of the way the Elizabethans perceived India? Consider in detail Shakespeare's choice of language and imagery in the extract.
- What links can you find between your analysis and the historical information given above on the creation of the East India Company?

> His mother was a votress[1] of my order,
> And in the spicèd Indian air by night
> Full often hath she gossiped by my side,
> And sat with me on Neptune's[2] yellow sands
> Marking th'embarkèd traders[3] on the flood,
> When we have laughed to see the sails conceive
> And grow big-bellied with the wanton[4] wind;
> Which she, with pretty and with swimming gait[5]
> Following (her womb then rich with my young squire),
> Would imitate, and sail upon the land
> To fetch me trifles, and return again
> As from a voyage, rich with merchandise.

Suggestions for Answer

Shakespeare's verse uses imagery extensively. Two central and complementary images are used: of fertility and of material wealth. Firstly, the two women laugh to see 'the sails conceive' as a result of which they 'grow big-bellied', a compound word used to convey the impression of pregnancy. However, this fruitfulness is not produced from within a marriage but as a result of the alliterative 'wanton wind',

----

1 Worshipper, member of religious order
2 Greek god of the sea
3 Traders who had set sail
4 Immoral, mischievous
5 Gliding movement

the word 'wanton' giving the impression that this is fun, light-hearted and immoral. This is also endorsed by the verb 'laughed'. This imagery relates specifically to the 'embarked traders' i.e. those who have come to trade for Indian goods. However, this image is then linked to the Indian woman herself whose womb is 'rich' and who then journeys to 'sail upon the land' and returns 'rich with merchandise'. This is said to 'imitate' the traders who have arrived. These images are also linked to the adjective 'spiced' which is used to describe India at the beginning of the extract. Thus, India is perceived as a place of wealth and fruitfulness, but a place of different moral values including, here, a strong sense of female solidarity.

Shakespeare and History

Within its historical context, there are several possible interpretations of this extract. There is clearly a correlation between India and trade and particularly the spices that form a central part of this. On the one hand, the traders are viewed in a sexual way and the riches they seek are linked to human fertility as their vessels 'conceive' (this connection is made explicit in the description of the woman's baby as 'rich'). This is a beautiful and romantic image of the relationship between coloniser and colonised. However, there is a more disturbing undercurrent and another possible reading. The light-heartedness of the union may indicate lack of responsibility on the part of the traders. The difference in the moral values of India has led to the traders taking advantage for their own ultimate gain. This is closely linked to the Indian woman herself. She imitates the actions of the traders and serves Titania by fetching trifles for her from land, another reflection of the relationship between colonised and coloniser. Arguably, Titania at least tries to accept her responsibilities by looking after the child – although the end of the play sees her relinquish him to Oberon so her bond with the Indian woman was finally fragile, appearing only to serve her own interests. In an evocative passage of poetic writing, Shakespeare has represented India as beautiful and exotic but also as female and at a time when women were straightforwardly the property of their husbands, this power relation is closely linked to events in colonial history.

Extension work – thinking about post-colonial theory

Some early post-colonial theorists claim that western writers portrayed India by a series of oppositions, i.e. qualities exhibited by the western character are exactly the opposite to qualities exhibited by the Indian character. So, for example, the west is portrayed in stereotypically masculine terms as rational, scientific, strong, decisive and paternal whereas India is portrayed as intuitive, imaginative, weak, indecisive and maternal. Later critics have challenged this reading as too simplistic, but you might consider this theory in relation to the Shakespeare extract in the previous exercise. How far is India represented in this extract as one side of an opposition? If we accept this reading, then how do we interpret the western traders who are only briefly mentioned but whose qualities, by opposition, may be deduced?

Exercise 2

Trade with India is now reflected symbolically in modern supermarkets, full of Indian products from sauces to snacks. In this exercise, we will consider how Shakespeare's representation of India as a trading partner replete with unbounded riches continues into the twenty-first century.

Look at the following extracts taken from Figure 4.1, the packaging for Veetee Basmati rice available commercially.

- What impression does the language in these texts create of India and Indian food?

Veetee Supreme Basmati

Harvested in the foothills of the Himalayas and carefully matured to achieve the perfect flavour, the flagship of the Veetee range is distinctively aromatic with an exquisite flavour, delicate texture and elegant grain length on cooking. A truly supreme Basmati.

The rice of life.

Supreme Vintage Basmati – Limited Edition

In India, special occasions demand the best, and honoured guests will be served matured Basmati. Like the best champagnes, the secret of Veetee Supreme Vintage Basmati is specially selected grains, aged to perfection for over 2 years since harvesting in the traditional manner. This guarantees grains with a beautiful milky white appearance, extra grain length and superior separation in addition to the characteristic sweetness and aroma of the best pure Basmati. Take time to savour the classic qualities of this matured rice, designed to complement special meals with friends and family.

Figure 4.1 The packaging of Veetee Basmati rice in 2003
Reproduced by courtesy of Veetee Rice Ltd

Suggestions for Answer

The primary semantic field endorses the notion of richness and uniqueness. The use of the word 'vintage' conjures images of fine wine, endorsed by the simile 'like the best champagnes'. The idea of uniqueness is emphasised with the adjective 'best' while the image also evokes connotations of festivity and celebration. The idea that the rice is very special is emphasised in both texts by use of lexis such as 'perfection', 'exquisite' and 'supreme'. One brand is additionally referred to as 'Limited Edition', an unusual and striking image taken from the field of art and further conveying the uniqueness of the rice. This also links to the adjective 'elegant'. Yet, interestingly, although the impact of these words creates an impression that the rice is not simply a basic foodstuff (the word 'delicate' emphasises this), the slogan 'the rice of life', used in the first text, implies that, in spite of the product's uniqueness, it is not solely restricted to special occasions. This is explicitly contrasted with the 'supreme vintage', produced for 'special meals'.

Another semantic field is that of tradition and age. The word 'matured' is used in both texts and is coupled with lexis such as 'vintage', 'classic' and 'aged'. The reader is invited, via an **imperative**, to 'take time' to 'savour' this special product. The exotic origins of the product are highlighted by the reference to the Himalayas in the first text. Indeed, the very name of the company ('Veetee') sounds like an Indian name (although, in fact, it isn't), further endorsing the product's exotic appeal. In all, language is used in a creative and effective way to persuade an audience to purchase this product; just as the Elizabethans were drawn to the richness of Indian culture, the same attraction holds for a twenty-first-century consumer. The commercial context remains, but updated here for a modern supermarket audience.

ROMANTICISM AND INDIA

India continued to offer a fascinating topic for western writers, some of whom also held administrative positions for the East India Company or served with the company's army in India. By the late eighteenth/early nineteenth centuries, a new group of poets had established themselves who are now called 'the Romantics'. Samuel Taylor Coleridge had been one of the early group of Romantic poets and much of his work sought to explore experiences beyond our daily, familiar reality; poems such as *The Rime of the Ancient Mariner* took the story's hero on a strange and exotic journey to the South Pole where he experienced supernatural visitations far-removed from his ordinary life on shore. Coleridge was a significant influence on Mary Shelley who was later to write *Frankenstein*, another Romantic work where extreme settings such as the frozen Arctic wastes form a backdrop for extraordinary experience. This notion of extreme experience has been called 'the sublime'. Romantic works also often involve a lonely and isolated individual at odds with the world and seeking self-knowledge.

Among the later Romantics, Percy Bysshe Shelley often expressed his fascination with the exotic by using India as a subject or setting for his poems. His cousin, Thomas Medwin, served with the East India Company's army for five years and his good friend the novelist Thomas Love Peacock was a senior bureaucrat at their offices in London. The following extract is taken from the poem *Alastor; or the Spirit of Solitude* first published by P. B. Shelley in 1816.

Exercise 3

Read the following text from Shelley's *Alastor*. It is written over two hundred years later than Shakespeare's text. What differences and similarities can you notice in the way India is represented in Shelley's poem compared to Shakespeare's play?

> The Poet wandering on, through Arabie[1]
> And Persia, and the wild Carmanian[2] waste,
> And o'er the aerial mountains which pour down
> Indus[3] and Oxus,[4] from their icy caves,
> In joy and exultation held his way;
> Till in the vale of Cashmire,[5] far within
> Its loneliest dell, where odorous plants entwine
> Beneath the hollow rocks a natural bower,
> Beside a sparkling rivulet he stretched
> His languid limbs. A vision on his sleep
> There came, a dream of hopes that never yet
> Had flushed his cheek. He dreamed a veilèd maid
> Sate near him, talking in low solemn tones.
> Her voice was like the voice of his own soul
> Heard in the calm of thought; its music long,
> His inmost sense suspended in its web
> Of many-coloured woof and shifting hues.
> Knowledge and truth and virtue were her theme,
> And lofty hopes of divine liberty,
> Thoughts the most dear to him and poesy,
> Herself a poet.

---

1 Modern Arabia, now a peninsula comprising a range of Arab states such as Kuwait, Saudi Arabia, Yemen, etc.
2 A region in the Middle East in modern Iran
3 A river that runs through Kashmir, originally part of the northern territory of British India
4 Ancient name of the modern river Amu Darya on the borders of modern Afghanistan
5 Modern Kashmir

Suggestions for Answer

This poem follows the wanderings of the isolated poet as he seeks the source of his own poetic inspiration and his journey takes him to the East (not, though, in first person but told in third person). Setting is much more geographically specific in this text where places and rivers are named, although using names that are archaic and poetic. Adjectives used to describe these places give a keen impression of the sublime with 'wild', 'icy' and 'loneliest' (the superlative adjective here emphasising that this is a place of extremes). The East as a place becomes a composite here of Indian and Persian locations that appear to be mingled together. Shelley never visited the East, so this geographical location is very much one of his own imagination. The use of the proper noun 'Arabie' is imprecise and conjures more an image of *The Arabian Nights* (a series of tales first translated into English in 1708, so well-known in the nineteenth century) than a specific location. The place is seen as both exotic and natural: 'odorous', 'natural', 'sparkling' and rivers and water are central to this. The East created here is lush and rich. Nature is a reviving and healing place for the poet. Yet, like Shakespeare's text, India is also linked with the feminine, reflected in the dream vision of a female poet with images taken from other arts such as music and spinning.

Shelley and History

Although there are some similarities with Shakespeare's text (the richness of India and the female spirit of poetry who resides there), there are also some key differences. Shelley's focus is far beyond any mention of commercial relations and his use of the East is for his Romantic poet to find himself. The East is represented as a place of untouched and lush nature which gives access to a place of dreams and poetry. Yet, ironically, Shelley was writing at a time when the East India Company was at its most powerful and, in 1821, Shelley wrote to his friend Thomas Love Peacock asking for a job there. Shelley himself claimed that he was not interested in the East as such but simply used it as a suitable setting for an **allegorical** work about poetry. In fact, later in the poem, the poet is warned against sacrificing real human love for this dream vision; an allegory on the importance of communion with others through life. In this reading, the East becomes an exotic and attractive yet destructive force. Perhaps this reflects a more mature colonial vision than Shakespeare's where the East no longer straightforwardly offers riches for the West but a more troubled and complex temptation away from western values?

CONSUMPTION AND THE EAST

As we have seen, in the early days of the East India Company, some of the representations of India focused explicitly on trade relations with the country. During the Romantic period, this changed, although the influence of the Company could still perhaps be seen behind the façade created by Romantic poets.

In this exercise, we will look more specifically at the idea of consumption by looking at food. Indian food has always been of interest to the West and the following texts focus on curry, the quintessentially Indian dish for any western mind. The word 'curry' is a **borrowing** from the Indian language Tamil where '*kari*' means 'sauce'. Employees of the East India Company began to want to eat curry when they returned home and, in 1809, the first Indian restaurant opened in London. Eliza Acton, a Victorian cookery writer, published six new recipes in 1845 and Queen Victoria was known to have included curry on the palace's menu.

Exercise 4

Text A is taken from the novel *Vanity Fair* by William Makepeace Thackeray, first published in book form in 1848; Text B is taken from the novel *White Teeth* by Zadie Smith first published in 2000.

- Compare these two texts and their representation of India. Both are set in England but take the symbol of curry as their central concern.
- Consider what perspective these texts come from and compare how this creates power relations in the two novels. As far as you can, try and link this to the times when the two novels were written.

In Text A, Joseph Sedley is an employee of the East India Company posted in India. He has recently returned for a period of leave in England, staying with his parents in London. He there meets Becky Sharp, friend of his sister Amelia, and she is invited back to the family home for a meal.

In Text B, Ardashir runs an Indian restaurant in England. Here, he gives advice to his waiters prior to the restaurant's busy period.

Suggestions for answer are at the back of the book.

Text A

Now we have heard how Mrs Sedley had prepared a fine curry for her son, just as he liked it, and in the course of dinner a portion of this dish was offered to Rebecca. 'What is it?' said she, turning an appealing look to Mr Joseph.

'Capital,' said he. His mouth was full of it; his face quite red with the delightful exercise of gobbling. 'Mother, it's as good as my own curries in India.'

'Oh, I must try some, if it is an Indian dish,' said Miss Rebecca. 'I am sure everything must be good that comes from there.'

'Give Miss Sharp some curry, my dear,' said Mr Sedley, laughing.

Rebecca had never tasted the dish before.

'Do you find it as good as everything from India?' said Mr Sedley.

---

continued

'Oh, excellent!' said Rebecca, who was suffering tortures with the cayenne pepper.

'Try a chili with it, Miss Sharp,' said Joseph, really interested.

'A chili,' said Rebecca, gasping. 'O yes!' She thought a chili was something cool, as its name imported, and was served with some. 'How fresh and green they look!' she said, and put some into her mouth. It was hotter than the curry; flesh and blood could bear it no longer. She laid down her fork. 'Water, for Heaven's sake, water!' she cried. Mr Sedley burst out laughing (he was a coarse man, from the Stock Exchange, where they love all sorts of practical jokes). 'They are real Indian, I assure you,' said he. 'Sambo, give Miss Sharp some water.'

Text B

A few hours later Ardashir appeared once more through the swing doors, breaking up the singing to deliver his second-phase pep talk. 'Gentlemen, gentlemen! That is more than enough of that. Now, listen up: it's ten-thirty. They've seen the show. They're hungry. They only got one pitiful tub of ice-cream in the interval and plenty of Bombay gin, which, as we all know, brings on the need for curry and that, gentlemen, is where we come in. Two tables of fifteen came in and sat at the back. Now: when they ask for water what do you do? What do you do, Ravind?' Ravind was brand new, nephew of the chef, sixteen, nervy. 'You tell them – '

'No, Ravind, even before you speak, what do you do?'

Ravind bit his lip. 'I don't know, Ardashir.'

'*You shake your head*,' said Ardashir, shaking his head. 'Simultaneous with a look of concern and fear for their well-being.' Ardashir demonstrated the look. 'And then you say?'

'Water does not help the heat, sir.'

'But what helps the heat, Ravind? What will aid the gentleman with the burning sensation he is presently feeling?'

'More rice, Ardashir.'

'And? And?'

Ravind looked stumped and began to sweat. Samad, who had been belittled by Ardashir too many times to enjoy watching someone else play the victim, leant over to whisper the answer in Ravind's clammy ear.

Ravind's face lit up in gratitude. 'More naan bread, Ardashir!'

'Yes, because it soaks up the chilli and more importantly water is free and naan bread is one pound twenty.'

Thackeray, Smith and History

Thackeray was writing at a time when English imperialism was at its height, although there had been much debate about the nature of government in India. Many had already begun to criticise the way the East India Company appeared to be interested only in commercial exploitation and their law-keeping forces served only to protect British merchants operating in India. Some of these critics believed that England had a responsibility to govern India for the welfare of Indians, not just the merchants, and religious bodies joined this debate urging the necessity for any government to take account of the spiritual and moral welfare of the governed. In 1813, some restraints had already been placed on the East India Company's monopoly and they were given additional responsibilities to allow missionaries into India and effect some social changes. However, there remained a feeling that the Company was only really interested in trade and profit. It could be argued that the portrayal of the Sedleys reflects these anxieties. If the colonisers were greedy, vulgar and motivated only by commercial gain, then this did not bode well for the future of India.

Smith is writing at the beginning of the twenty-first century and looking back on a century of change. India became independent in 1947 and the following years saw a rise in immigration to England from its former colonies. This created the multicultural society that we recognise as England today. Smith's characters are part of this fabric, showing initially those who have immigrated but moving to those who were born in England. The Indian restaurant scene shows this change and the ironic reversal of Indians coming to England to make money. The changed perspective shows an awareness of a world where England and English customs cannot be assumed to be the centre of the universe.

INDIA AND CONFLICT

Times of war and international conflict always provide interesting material for any cultural historian or literary critic because works produced often have an even clearer sense of values and attitudes. India continued to conduct its relations with England via the East India Company until 1858, so until this time, links with the country were characterised almost solely by trading concerns. The Company sought to intervene in the country's affairs only so far as commercial concerns would benefit from this. For example, a British education system was introduced during the 1830s emphasising the English language, culture and traditions so that the Company could educate its own local manpower rather than bear the cost of transporting workers from England. Clearly, the message given with this was that British culture was in every way superior. In 1857, it became clear that Indians would not continue to tolerate this. A series of local insurrections broke out in India, usually referred to as the Indian Mutiny and starting from the Indian soldiers in the British army called sepoys. The fighting soon escalated into horrific levels of violence and terrible retaliations on both sides. What particularly struck those in England who were following the reports was the ferocity that the mutineers exercised on the English women and children who were accompanying their husbands in India. Politicians used these images as justification to take full imperial control of India and when the Mutiny had ended, in 1858, the East India Company was disbanded and India became a Crown Colony.

Exercise 5

Look at the following two texts, both of which represent a specific moment in the history of the Mutiny when one of the besieged towns was rescued by a division of Highland soldiers.

Text A is from Tennyson's 1858 poem, *The Defence of Lucknow*. It is important that you remember that, in 1850, Tennyson was made Poet Laureate so had an official responsibility to portray national events. Text B is from a modern work by George MacDonald Fraser called *Flashman in the Great Game* which also retells events from the Mutiny. This was published in 1975.

- What attitudes and values do these texts convey?
- In particular, how do these texts represent English (and, indeed, Scottish) identity?
- In what ways have these texts modified the historical material to reflect the attitudes and values of their own context?

Suggestions for answer are not provided for this exercise.

Text A

All on a sudden the garrison utter a jubilant shout,
Havelock's[1] glorious Highlanders answer with conquering cheers,
Sick from the hospital echo them, women and children come out,
Blessing the wholesome white faces of Havelock's good fusileers,[2]
Kissing the war-harden'd hand of the Highlander wet with their tears!
Dance to the pibroch![3] – saved! we are saved! – is it you? is it you?
Saved by the valour of Havelock, saved by the blessing of Heaven!
'Hold it for fifteen days!' we have held it for eighty-seven![4]
And ever aloft on the palace roof the old banner of England blew.

---

1 Brigadier-General Henry Havelock who led the relief
2 Archaic spelling of 'fusilier' i.e. a soldier armed with a light musket
3 Melody played by a bagpipe
4 1700 men defended the British Residency of Lucknow against over 8000 mutineers. The mutiny began in Lucknow on 30 May and a temporary victory was achieved on 25 September, although fighting began again and a final victory wasn't achieved until 17 November. Havelock died on 24 November.

Text B

I knew it was as good as over when Billy Russell of *The Times* showed up to join Campbell's[1] final march on Lucknow – it's a sure sign of victory when the correspondents gather like vultures. We marched with 30,000 men and strong artillery, myself piling up great heaps of useless paper in Mansfield's intelligence section and keeping out of harm's way. It was an inexorable, pounding business, as our gunners blew the pandy[2] defences systematically to bits, the Highlanders and Irish slaughtered the sepoy infantry wherever it stood, the engineers demolished shrines and temples to show who was master, and everyone laid hands on as much loot as he could carry.

It was a great bloody carnival, with everyone making the most of the war: I recall one incident, in a Lucknow courtyard (I believe it may have been in the Begum's[3] palace) in which I saw Highlanders, their gory bayonets laid aside, smashing open chests that were simply stuffed with jewels, and grinning idiot little Goorkhas[4] breaking mirrors for sheer sport and wiping their knives on silks and fabrics worth a fortune.

Extension exercise

The following poem is another direct response to the events of the Mutiny, this time by a female poet, Christina Rossetti. It was published in 1862 and this is the complete poem.

- Compare this poem with the Tennyson extract above. What differences and similarities do you notice? Do you think that gender differences of the two poets have contributed to this?

---

1 Sir Colin Campbell, another of the military leaders at the relief of Lucknow
2 A colloquial name for any mutineer, derived from Mangal Pande, the sepoy who is usually cited as the man who started the Mutiny in Barrackpore
3 Muslim noblewoman or lady of high rank
4 Special regiment in the British army consisting of men from Nepal famed for their special military prowess

'In the Round Tower at Jhansi, June 8, 1857'

A hundred, a thousand to one; even so;
Not a hope in the world remained:
The swarming howling wretches below
Gained and gained and gained.
Skene looked at his pale young wife:-
'Is the time come?' – 'The time is come!' –
Young, strong, and so full of life:
The agony struck them dumb.

Close his arm about her now,
Close her cheek to his,
Close the pistol to her brow –
God forgive them this!

'Will it hurt much?' – 'No, mine own:
I wish I could bear the pang for both.'
'I wish I could bear the pang alone:
Courage, dear, I am not loth.'

Kiss and kiss: 'It is not pain
Thus to kiss and die.
One kiss more.' – 'And yet one again.' –
'Good bye.' – 'Good bye.'

SUMMARY

This chapter has done the following:

- Extended the notion of regional identity to a global framework
- Defined some aspects of post-colonial theory
- Applied these ideas to a range of texts

GENRES OVER TIME

In chapter 1, we discussed the various factors that shape the production of a text and this exploration has been extended in the following chapters to consider specific features in relation to texts from different periods. As part of this process, we have considered issues of genre when relevant. In this chapter, however, the notion of genre will be examined more closely, in particular as a means of considering the ways in which a society's attitudes and values can be reflected in the very form of a text.

Genres are different types of cultural products where certain expectations are created about the form of the work. In English studies, the big genres are usually recognised as poetry, prose and drama and yet within these broad headings there are numerous further divisions that can be made. To define a genre, we have to see various *similarities* between texts. For example, sonnets are defined in a very specific way as having fourteen lines of poetic writing using a variety of rhyme schemes. However, this variety of rhyme schemes already sets up *differences*: so-called Shakespearian and Petrarchan sonnets use different patterns of rhyme, giving different structures to the poems. This, then, provides a clear sub-genre within the broader genre of sonnet form. Extending this further, writers of sonnets, such as Shakespeare, rarely slavishly follow a fixed pattern even where they can be assigned to a distinct sub-genre. Shakespeare's sonnet sequence uses a range of rhythmical variations and includes sonnets of both fifteen (Sonnet 99) and twelve lines (Sonnet 126). In one sense, every text is a new genre as it will be fundamentally different to anything before it; however, for the sake of organisation and analysis, it is often useful to see similarities between texts and, in particular, to explore the impact different historical contexts can have on these genres.

(There is a more detailed consideration of genre in Adrian Beard's *The Language of Literature* in this series.)

TRAGEDY: THE DEVELOPMENT OF A GENRE

An exploration of the way tragedy has developed as a genre is a perfect illustration of the way historical contexts affect and change the form of a text. Tragedy has a very long and complex history and has been used in a variety of ways by writers, each individual writer developing the genre and adding additional flavour to the form. Tragedy began with the Ancient Greeks and an early attempt to define the genre can be found in the *Poetics*, a work by Aristotle, the Greek philosopher and early literary critic.

In essence, then, classical tragedy has the following characteristics:

- Is a dramatic representation conveyed in poetic language
- Depicts the misfortunes that befall human beings
- Usually centres on a tragic hero, defined by Aristotle as a noble, male character who is involved in serious events often with broader social and political repercussions
- This tragic hero has many good qualities, but also a fatal flaw leading to a major error of judgement which hastens the tragic events
- The journey to disaster and loss has an inevitable feel about it; the tragic hero usually has a moment of insight just before his death which makes the ending even more poignant
- The spectator experiences a sense of relief in witnessing such great suffering (this is called **catharsis**)

Aristotle based his definition of tragedy on the works of the Greek tragedians – Aeschylus, Sophocles and Euripides – which were available to him.

The Elizabethan age saw a great flourishing of drama and, the Renaissance being a time when Greek and Roman learning was given high status, Aristotle's laws for tragedy can be perceived in many of the plays of that time – although remember that every individual writer will have their own way of engaging with this.

Exercise 1

Read the following text which is taken from the end of Shakespeare's tragedy *King Lear*, first published in 1605. Taking Aristotle's definition of tragedy, how far would you say that Shakespeare's play exhibits the characteristics of this genre?

The play focuses on Lear's foolishness and the poor judgements he makes about people as a result. Earlier in the play, he has unwisely rejected his good daughter, Cordelia, thereby placing himself at the mercy of his other two unscrupulous daughters. At the end of the play, Lear, wiser after his sufferings, is reunited with Cordelia only to be parted again almost immediately when she is murdered.

LEAR:	Howl, howl, howl, howl! O, you are men of stones.
	Had I your tongues and eyes, I'd use them so,
	That heaven's vault should crack. She's gone for ever.
	I know when one is dead and when one lives.
	She's dead as earth.

> [*He lays her down.*]
>
> Lend me a looking-glass;[1]
> If that her breath will mist or stain the stone,
> Why then she lives.
>
> KENT: Is this the promised end?
> EDGAR: Or image of that horror?
> ALBANY: Fall and cease.
> LEAR: This feather stirs, she lives: if it be so,
> It is a chance which does redeem all sorrows
> That ever I have felt.
> KENT: O my good master!
> LEAR: Prithee, away.
> EDGAR: 'Tis noble Kent, your friend.
> LEAR: A plague upon you murderers, traitors all.
> I might have saved her; now she's gone for ever.

Suggestions for Answer

In many ways, it is possible to detect characteristics of the traditional tragedy in this extract. Looking at the definition given previously, we can see the following:

- This is a dramatic representation written in unrhymed iambic pentameters (**blank verse**), the verse form used by the Elizabethans in their plays.
- Clearly, the focus is on misfortune and suffering. Lear's anguish is conveyed through the simplicity and repetitiveness of his language ('Howl, howl, howl, howl!') rather than through complex imagery or verse forms. Midway through this extract he suddenly feels that Cordelia may be still alive, but this is countered by the end with his 'now she's gone for ever'.
- The focus is on a king and the royal family. Not only is the play about family relationships, but also about the government of England (and, in this case, a concern that the contemporary audience would share – the chaos that ensues when the kingdom is divided).
- Lear's foolishness does bring about these events, although he remains a sympathetic character. Even in this scene, you may feel that his sorrow, though poignant, is self-absorbed and leads him to abuse those around him as 'murderers' and 'traitors'. This sense of human failings is an important aspect of tragedy.

---

1 One way of interpreting this is that Lear wants to check whether Cordelia is alive by seeing if her breath creates mist on a mirror

- Having rejected Cordelia earlier in the play, Lear comes to understand, through his suffering, the value of honesty and simplicity. In this play, genuine emotion is conveyed through simple language and those who use language in a complex way are those who manipulate for their own ends. Unfortunately, the tragedy can only have its full effect if this realisation comes too late, as here. Shortly after this passage, Lear himself dies.
- The concept of catharsis is a difficult one for a modern audience. It is hard to say that we feel relieved at this point in the play, although this play can be exceptionally moving on the stage and by the end it is possible to feel emotionally exhausted. Is this what Aristotle meant? Through suffering, society has renewed itself even at the expense of particular individuals. Is this the primary focus by the end?

This study of Shakespeare's play, although brief, has raised some questions about the nature of tragedy and the way it was used by the Elizabethan and Jacobean dramatists.

Over the next one hundred years, both the social and political context and the theatres themselves changed almost beyond recognition. Shakespeare's original play presented problems for these later audiences and, in 1681, Nahum Tate rewrote the play making some very significant changes. The following exercise looks at this development of tragic form.

Exercise 2

This text comes from the end of Nahum Tate's rewritten *King Lear*. Don't worry too much about who the individual characters are; focus on understanding the feeling created by such a conclusion to the play.

- How has the atmosphere and focus of the play been changed by Tate?
- Do you have any suggestions why Tate would have wanted to make these changes?
- Which version do you prefer?

LEAR:	But, Edgar, I defer thy Joys[1] too long:
	Thou serv'd distress'd Cordelia; take her Crown'd
	Th'imperial Grace fresh blooming on her Brow;
	Nay, Gloster, Thou hast here a Father's Right,
	Thy helping Hand t' heap Blessings on their Heads.
KENT:	Old Kent throws in his hearty Wishes too.
EDGAR:	The Gods and You too largely recompense
	What I have done; the Gift strikes Merit dumb.
CORDELIA:	Nor do I blush to own my self o'er-paid
	For all my Suff'rings past.
GLOSTER:	Now, gentle Gods, give Gloster his Discharge.
LEAR:	No, Gloster, Thou hast Business yet for Life;
	Thou, Kent and I, retir'd to some cool Cell
	Will gently pass our short reserves of Time
	In calm Reflection on our Fortunes past,
	Cheer'd with Relation of the prosperous Reign
	Of this celestial Pair; Thus our Remains
	Shall in an even Course of Thought be past,
	Enjoy the present Hour, nor fear the Last.
EDGAR:	Our drooping Country now erects her Head,
	Peace spreads her balmy Wings, and Plenty blooms.
	Divine Cordelia, all the Gods can Witness
	How much thy Love to Empire I prefer!
	Thy bright Example shall convince the World
	(Whatever Storms of Fortune are decreed)
	That Truth and Virtue shall at last succeed.

Suggestions for Answer

This version has been changed by Tate to avoid completely the atmosphere of tragedy that we found in Shakespeare's version. Everyone is alive by the end of the play, the older characters retire to a contented time of reflection while the younger are married and prepare to renew the 'drooping country' for a time of peace. The prevailing atmosphere of this ending is peace, harmony and resolution. The final moral emphasises that those who do good will be rewarded, a very

---

1 During the seventeenth century, capitals were not only used at the beginning of sentences, but on nouns that were important. This became more widespread and by the eighteenth century books appeared in which all or most of the nouns were given an initial capital (much like modern German). Works by eighteenth-century writers (Swift, Pope, etc.) are full of these capitals. In the later eighteenth century, grammar books began to appear which discouraged the practice and it became less frequent.

straightforward moral universe completely different to the harsher, more arbitrary world of Shakespeare's play.

Tate and History

To understand why Tate made these changes, it is important to have some knowledge of what happened between 1605 and 1681. The intervening years had witnessed the English Civil War, the execution of King Charles I, Cromwell's Commonwealth when the theatres were all closed down and, finally, the Restoration of the monarchy under King Charles II in 1660. Many critics have made explicit comparisons between the time when Shakespeare was writing and the huge changes that began to develop from 1660. Shakespeare's age is often characterised as a time of questioning and unrest and many critics have interpreted Shakespeare's tragedies as an artistic expression of this time of unease. Eventually, this unease and the ideological conflicts that were growing led to the Civil War. The Restoration, alternatively, became a time of facts rather than speculation and a new kind of society began to emerge that was predominantly Protestant, middle-class and politically stable. Reason, control, tradition and harmony became the guiding principles rather than the emotion and intellectual challenge of the Renaissance. Even the theatres of the Restoration were different from Shakespeare's theatre, moving to indoor venues, more expensive tickets and a largely upper-class audience. What were seen as the emotional excesses of Shakespeare's writing had to be rewritten to make them acceptable for a Restoration audience. The restoration of order and the monarchy at the end of Tate's version was particularly relevant for an audience enjoying the return of their own monarchy. The Restoration audience had had enough of suffering and demanded happy endings and **comedy**. Comedy became the major genre during this period.

Critics have generally commented on the superiority of Shakespeare's version and you may well have preferred this one in your own reading. However, it is important to understand that both of these texts have emerged from a specific set of historical, social and political conditions and the tragic genre itself has been modified to reflect this. Many critics have explained our modern preference for Shakespeare's version as the fact that we live during an age that has more in common with the Elizabethans than with the Restoration. Certainly, it appears to be true that the value we put on questioning and challenging accepted truths may make us more Shakespeare's contemporaries than Tate's.

TRAGEDY AS COMEDY

Exercise 3

The next two examples take the idea of tragedy but re-present the genre in a comic mode.

Read the two texts and consider how they both undermine the seriousness of tragedy by re-presenting tragic ideas in a comic way. Text A is taken from a passage directly after *The Monk's Tale* in Chaucer's *The Canterbury Tales* (begun in 1386 and never completed), here given in Nevill Coghill's translation from the original Middle English, first published in 1951. The Monk has just finished telling his tale which has involved detailing a series of tragic stories, or as the Monk himself says, 'I have some tragedies to tell; I have at least a hundred in my cell'. The Monk has earlier defined tragedy and this forms the basis for the selection of his tales:

> a certain kind of story
> As old books tell, of those who fell from glory,
> People that stood in great prosperity
> And were cast down out of their high degree
> Into calamity, and so they died.

Text B is taken from Willy Russell's play *Educating Rita*, first performed by the Royal Shakespeare Company in 1980. Rita, a working-class hairdresser, embarks on an Open University course with her tutor, Frank; here, they are discussing a recent production of *Macbeth* that Rita has seen.

• Discuss the assumptions about tragedy that are being presented in these two texts. What is the effect of creating comedy out of essentially tragic material?

Text A

Our Host joined in. 'This Monk, he talks too loud;
I don't know what – and as for "Tragedy",
You heard just now, what has to be must be.
It does no good to grumble and complain,
What's done is done. Moreover, it's a pain,
As you have said, to hear about disaster;
Let's have no more of it. God bless you, master,
It's an offence, you're boring us, that's why!
Such talk as that's not worth a butterfly,
Gives no enjoyment, doesn't help the game.
In short Sir Monk – Sir Peter – what's-your-name –
I heartily beg you'll talk of something else.'

Text B

RITA   [*moving towards the door*]: Well, I better get back. I've left a customer with a perm lotion. If I don't get a move on there'll be another tragedy.

FRANK: No. There won't be a tragedy.

RITA: There will, y' know. I know this woman; she's dead fussy. If her perm doesn't come out right there'll be blood an' guts everywhere.

FRANK: Which might be quite tragic –

[*He throws her the apple from his desk which she catches.*]

– but it won't be a tragedy.

RITA: What?

FRANK: Well – erm – look; the tragedy of the drama has nothing to do with the sort of tragic event you're talking about. Macbeth is flawed by his ambition – yes?

RITA   [*going and sitting in the chair by the desk*]: Yeh. Go on.

[*She starts to eat the apple.*]

FRANK: Erm – it's the flaw which forces him to take the inevitable step towards his own doom. You see?

[RITA *offers him the can of soft drink. He takes it and looks at it.*]

FRANK   [*putting the can down on the desk*]: No thanks. Whereas, Rita, a woman's hair being reduced to an inch of stubble, or – or the sort of thing you read in the paper that's reported as being tragic, 'Man Killed by Falling Tree', is not a tragedy.

RITA: It is for the poor sod under the tree.

Suggestions for Answer

Chaucer's medieval text comes from a time when Aristotle's definition of tragedy was largely unknown. The Monk's definition of tragedy helps the reader to see exactly what the medieval conception of the genre was: the story of a wealthy and noble man who falls from this position into one of great misery which ends in death. Aristotle's idea of a fatal flaw has little relevance here, but more significant is the image of Fortune's Wheel, a popular image of the time which symbolised the fact that everyone who is elevated to a high position is subject, by the revolution of the wheel, to a corresponding fall in due course. Chaucer creates humour by having the Host interrupt the Monk, begging him to end his miserable stories. This certainly challenges our normal idea of tragedy (derived from Aristotle) as something lofty and serious. The light-heartedness of *The Canterbury Tales* has no place for such depressing stories. The comic feeling is enhanced by the jaunty use of rhyming couplets and the regular **iambic metre**.

Willy Russell's dramatic text continues this tradition of mocking high tragedy. Frank, the university tutor, attempts to give Rita an Aristotelian definition of tragedy, but this pretension is continually undermined by Rita's responses. This text similarly reflects its 1980 context. During the 1970s, educational opportunities for working-class people became more widespread. The establishment of the Open University in 1971 was designed to offer opportunities for those unable to take advantage of traditional university routes to gain an education where they could study for a degree with no formal entry qualifications. This created a great social change and many of those admitted to these places began to question the values of what may have been seen as the traditional establishment. Rita's lack of understanding about the conventionally accepted definition of tragedy is comic in two ways: firstly and most straightforwardly, by revealing the humour of her working-class background (much as many of Chaucer's jokes operate in *The Canterbury Tales*) and secondly, by forcing the audience to question the values reflected by Frank. The play stages a meeting between the two worlds from which both must derive benefit.

It is interesting that, in traditional classical criticism, tragedy has always been viewed as a much higher and more serious art-form than comedy. Yet, there are clearly certain ages that refuse to accept this hierarchy. Perhaps it could be read that Chaucer's medieval age, the eighteenth century when Nahum Tate was rewriting *King Lear* and the twentieth century were, for various and different reasons, less comfortable with the serious, Aristotelian version of a tragic work. Often **satire** is given a corresponding status in all these societies. It is important, however, to remember that these are broad generalisations, even though it is possible to detect these kinds of pattern.

A MODERN TRAGEDY

The last section raised the issue of tragedy in a modern age and this returns us to our discussion in Chapter 1 where we explored Ibsen's play *A Doll's House*, in particular looking at the fact that Ibsen called his work 'A Modern Tragedy'. What he meant by this was that he wanted to redefine the genre for his own use. His tragedy centred on a middle-class woman (not an aristocratic man), focused on ordinary domestic life (rather than the world of courts and high politics) and ended, not in literal physical death, but in the death of the main protagonist's old lifestyle. The play ended with renewal for society, just as in a traditional tragedy, although the ending was much more ambiguous and many audiences found Ibsen's original ending deeply unsettling. In one sense, Ibsen saw his own tragic works as concerned with exposing the truth and looking beyond a world of illusory happiness to a sadder, but enlightened, world representing 'reality'.

The twentieth century was certainly to take and develop this notion of tragedy further. One of the most famous writers who sought to write a modern tragedy was Arthur Miller.

Exercise 4

Read the following text from Arthur Miller's *Death of a Salesman* published in 1949. The central character, Willy Loman, has worked his whole life as a salesman, but has now lost his job. This extract occurs towards the end of the play when Willy's son, Biff, finally has an honest conversation with his father about their mutual lack of achievement. Happy is Willy's younger son and Linda is Willy's wife.

- In what way does this play both use and extend traditional tragic form?

WILLY   [*with hatred, threateningly*]: The door of your life is wide open!

BIFF: Pop! I'm a dime a dozen, and so are you!

WILLY   [*turning on him now in an uncontrolled outburst*]: I am not a dime a dozen! I am Willy Loman, and you are Biff Loman!

[BIFF *starts for* WILLY, *but is blocked by* HAPPY. *In his fury*, BIFF *seems on the verge of attacking his father.*]

BIFF: I am not a leader of men, Willy, and neither are you. You were never anything but a hard-working drummer who landed in the ash-can like all the rest of them! I'm one dollar an hour, Willy! I tried seven states and couldn't raise it. A buck an hour! Do you gather my meaning? I'm not bringing home any prizes any more, and you're going to stop waiting for me to bring them home!

WILLY   [*directly to* BIFF]: You vengeful, spiteful mut!

[BIFF *breaks away from* HAPPY. WILLY, *in fright, starts up the stairs.* BIFF *grabs him.*]

BIFF   [*at the peak of his fury*]: Pop, I'm nothing! I'm nothing, Pop. Can't you understand that? There's no spite in it any more. I'm just what I am, that's all.

[BIFF'*s fury has spent itself, and he breaks down, sobbing, holding on to* WILLY, *who dumbly fumbles for* BIFF'*s face.*]

WILLY   [*astonished*]: What're you doing? What're you doing? [*To* LINDA] Why is he crying?

BIFF   [*broken, crying*]: Will you let me go, for Christ's sake? Will you take that phony dream and burn it before something happens? [*Struggling to contain himself, he pulls away and moves to the stairs.*] I'll go in the morning. Put him – put him to bed.

[*Exhausted*, BIFF *moves up the stairs to his room.*]

WILLY   [*after a long pause, astonished, elevated*]: Isn't that – isn't that remarkable? Biff – he likes me!

Suggestions for Answer

Judged against the traditional definition of tragedy, you may analyse this extract in the following way.

Although this is clearly a dramatic text, it is not written in poetry but in prose. In fact, not only is it prose, but it is a colloquial, Americanised form of language with **clichés** such as 'dime a dozen' and specific Americanisms such as 'ash-can', 'dollar', 'buck', etc. The action is set at a particular time and place, one very remote from the classical world of tragedy and yet a world more relevant to the experience of modern readers.

The play is clearly about the misfortunes that befall a human being, but rather than great tragic themes, the misfortunes here appear more mundane and are about human failure on a much less glamorous level. (Though, on another level, *King Lear* was also about the conflicts and pressures of family life – especially sons and daughters – very similar to this play.)

The central tragic character is male, although he is certainly not noble. The status of the main protagonist is signalled in the title – a salesman – and his tragic fall may have little effect on the national political framework but is a personal tragedy. However, it could be argued that the commercial society that the play presents with its lack of human values does take Willy Loman's story to a much broader and more significant level.

You would probably need to be familiar with the play as a whole to be able to judge Willy Loman's character in greater depth. Rather than a great tragic figure with a fatal flaw, many critics see him simply as an ordinary man, undoubtedly flawed, but only on a mundane level; he is not heroic. Critics often view the hero of modern tragedies as an **anti-hero**, a character who is petty, ineffectual and passive, not dignified and powerful. This becomes tragedy for a modern age and Miller himself argued that tragedy should not be restricted to kings and queens. Tragedy is now the grief of the ordinary man or woman (consider also Ibsen).

Willy does have a moment of insight, and this extract from the play illustrates that. He comes to understand that there is a world of human love and emotion beyond the sterile successes of the material world of commerce. He also finally has to face the truth (one already seen by Biff) that he has fallen vastly short of his own ideals. For Willy, the only viable response to this is suicide. In classical tragedy, the process towards inevitable death is often marked by great passages of poetry to emphasise the suffering; however, in this play suffering is much less vocal, almost inarticulate. Again, perhaps this has something in common with Lear and Shakespeare himself, in the words 'howl, howl, howl, howl!', may also have been aware of the power of suffering beyond articulate expression.

Finally, as we have seen with Lear, the concept of catharsis is a difficult one for a modern audience. This becomes even more difficult with a modern tragedy such as this one. Perhaps it is more appropriate to think simply about compassion rather than catharsis? But then, as we have seen with the Lear discussion, perhaps this has always been the case?

TRAGEDY IN THE NOVEL

Another of the developments within tragedy as a genre in a modern context came about with the extension of the genre beyond the remit of drama. The following exercise looks more closely at novels that might be considered modern tragedies in the same way that *Death of a Salesman* might be.

Exercise 5

- How do these extracts reflect a translation of tragic form and atmosphere to the novel?
- What do you think might be significant about the dates when these novels were written?

Text A is taken from *Tess of the d'Urbervilles* by Thomas Hardy, published in 1891. The novel centres on Tess, a working-class West Country woman. This is the end of the novel after Tess has been executed for a crime of passion brought about by the circumstances of her life. The events that are described in Text A are witnessed from the point of view of Tess's sister and brother-in-law. Text B is taken from *Things Fall Apart* by Chinua Achebe, first published in 1958. This novel is set in Nigeria just before the advent of colonialism. The action of the novel is centred on Okonkwo who eventually hangs himself. Here, Okonkwo's friend, Obierika, discusses the situation with the white District Commissioner.

Suggestions for answer are at the back of the book.

Text A

Upon the cornice of the tower a tall staff was fixed. Their eyes were riveted on it. A few minutes after the hour had struck something moved slowly up the staff, and extended itself upon the breeze. It was a black flag.

'Justice' was done, and the President of the Immortals, in Aeschylean[1] phrase, had ended his sport with Tess. And the d'Urberville knights and dames slept on in their tombs unknowing.[2] The two speechless gazers bent themselves down to the earth, as if in prayer, and remained thus a long time, absolutely motionless: the flag continued to wave silently. As soon as they had strength they arose, joined hands again, and went on.

---

1 Aeschylus was a Greek writer of tragedies
2 The novel's tragic events are brought about by a discovery that Tess's family are related to the aristocratic d'Urberville family

'Will you bury him like any other man?' asked the Commissioner.

'We cannot bury him. Only strangers can. We shall pay your men to do it. When he has been buried we will then do our duty by him. We shall make sacrifices to cleanse the desecrated land.'

Obierika, who had been gazing steadily at his friend's dangling body, turned suddenly to the District Commissioner and said ferociously: 'That man was one of the greatest men in Umuofia. You drove him to kill himself; and now he will be buried like a dog . . . ' He could not say any more. His voice trembled and choked his words.

Extension exercise

In Rob Pope's *The English Studies Book*, he considers the Queen song 'Bohemian Rhapsody' (1975) as a tragedy from popular culture. Not only is this song known by a broad range of people, but it has also been parodied innumerable times, most memorably in the film *Wayne's World,* and has been used as a comic reference by Terry Pratchett. However, the death of Freddie Mercury, the lead singer of Queen, in 1991 of AIDS adds, according to Pope, to the song's tragic and mythic status.

This final exercise will encourage you to consider how tragedy has been reinterpreted for a twenty-first-century audience. The following text is taken from President George Bush's speech on 13 September 2001, two days after the terrorist attacks on the USA.

- What similarities and differences can you find with the other tragic works in this section?

Suggestions for answer are not provided for this exercise.

Civilized people around the world denounce the evildoers who devised and executed these terrible attacks. Justice demands that those who helped or harbored the terrorists be punished – and punished severely. The enormity of their evil demands it. We will use all the resources of the United States and our cooperating friends and allies to pursue those responsible for this evil, until justice is done.

We mourn with those who have suffered great and disastrous loss. All our hearts have been seared by the sudden and sense-less taking of innocent lives.

continued

We pray for healing and for the strength to serve and encourage one another in hope and faith.

Scripture says: 'Blessed are those who mourn for they shall be comforted.' I call on every American family and the family of America to observe a National Day of Prayer and Remembrance, honoring the memory of the thousands of victims of these brutal attacks and comforting those who lost loved ones. We will persevere through this national tragedy and personal loss. In time, we will find healing and recovery; and, in the face of all this evil, we remain strong and united, 'one Nation under God.'

SUMMARY

This chapter has done the following:

- Looked specifically at genre and its place in historical criticism
- Applied this by looking closely at the genre of tragedy
- Continued to develop analytical and critical skills

TAKING STOCK AND MOVING FORWARD

TEXT OR CONTEXT

The aim of this book has been to develop a deeper understanding of how to incorporate contextual material into the analysis of both literary and non-literary texts. The approach is intended to illustrate the best way to consider the influence of contextual factors with the prime focus being on the text itself; it has not been the intention to provide a historical list of literary and linguistic features that may be found within a specific historical period. In fact, it is hoped that the artificiality of such approaches has been highlighted and you will have a greater appreciation of the tentative and uncertain nature of any contextual interpretation. At the same time, as has been discussed, a text is produced from a specific society that has certain shared values and viewpoints and these may not necessarily be shared by the modern reader. The dynamics of interpretation come into play when these two factors – the producer and the reader – interact. The readings in this book are not intended to be fixed or final but are there merely to illustrate the stages that all readers are involved in during this process of interpretation. You may yourself uncover contextual material that conflicts with the readings offered here and may begin to consider alternative interpretations of your own.

However, although this dynamic is undoubtedly exciting, there are some pitfalls to be highlighted before you begin to put this method into practice. An obvious problem that students now face is how to maintain a balance between the text itself and its context. Looking at much of the critical work now being produced within the field of literary studies, you would be forgiven for thinking that some of these would not look out of place in the History department. There are no absolute or final answers on this, but it is important to remember that it is the text that is the primary object of study and contextual factors are used merely to assist the process of interpretation. If you find that the majority of your writing is spent detailing contextual features, then something is probably going wrong and you will not score highly. If, however, you can show that all texts have a close relationship with their contexts which help shape the way they are written and the views expressed within them, and can offer some tentative suggestions to show the influence that these have had on the text's final form, then you are probably writing something closer to a good answer. This will naturally lead you to consider contextual readings as one way of interpreting a text and creating meaning, not as an end in itself.

Perhaps the best way to illustrate this process and provide an appropriate conclusion is to look at a student essay. The following text is taken from an A2 English Literature student's essay and uses Robert Louis Stevenson's *The Strange Case of Dr Jekyll and Mr Hyde* as its central focus. This essay achieved a top band mark and illustrates clearly the kind of analysis that you should be aiming for. Read this extract carefully, highlighting as you read what you think are the successes of this essay. A list of its positive features is provided after the extract from an examiner's perspective.

At the time that Stevenson wrote *Dr Jekyll and Mr Hyde*, London, like Edinburgh, was also a divided city. Despite being one of the largest and richest cities in the entire world, it contained extremes of both wealth and poverty. The restrictions of the New Town and the freedom of the Old Town of Edinburgh are shown in Stevenson's description of London by Hyde's haunts, 'dingy neighbourhood' in comparison with Jekyll's residence, 'a square of ancient handsome houses'. The setting itself becomes a symbol of the duality of human nature and shows a world, very much like that of the Victorians, where middle-class society, with its emphasis on respectability, affluence and morality, contrasts with an alternative working-class world of freedom, poverty and crime. This is emphasised by imagery of light and darkness, where Hyde's 'nocturnal city', 'black winter morning', 'dismal quarter' and 'gross darkness' are contrasted with the feeble efforts to dispel the darkness by 'lamps which had never been extinguished'.

Positive features of this essay:

- Well-integrated use of both contextual and textual analysis. Reference is made briefly to Stevenson's own context and this is immediately related to the text. The priority here is given to textual analysis.
- Quotations from the text are seamlessly integrated to support the points being made.
- Close analysis of language (imagery, choice of vocabulary) is evident alongside larger analysis of the novel's formal features such as setting or juxtapositions.
- Even in this brief discussion, the student has taken the analysis further to begin to consider Stevenson's ideas, i.e. the duality of human nature.
- The writing is mature and sophisticated, but also clear.

SUGGESTIONS FOR ANSWER

CHAPTER 1, EXERCISE 3

This is an interesting text to analyse from a gender perspective. In terms of layout (or **graphology**), this text is dominated by the pictures and the enlarged heading. The picture conveys the impression of a harmonious, happy household where there are distinct gender relations (the woman is making tea while the man appears to be preparing to go outside perhaps to do the gardening). The focus is clearly on the woman (the smaller photograph has a focus on her over the man's shoulder) and the implication is that the kitchen is her realm where she has control. However, unlike the usual implication that this is a limiting life, the representation here is that this is 'pleasure', the word itself larger than the other words in the sub-heading and her smiling face in the picture endorsing this. The text emphasises this further by the pre-modifying adjective 'real' before 'pleasure', implying that this has more value than other pleasures. The text concludes with the claim that this is not just a transitory pleasure but 'pleasure for life'. Similarly, the **semantic field** of the text is based on emotion, emphasised by alliteration in 'heart of your home' and later with 'room you love'. The pronoun 'you' is clearly aimed at the female reader and is juxtaposed with the helpful 'we' which represents Magnet Kitchens. The gender focus of this pronoun is vague in the text, but is, by implication, centred on the female by the positioning and focus in the pictures.

Class is also clearly an issue. The room implies a comfortable middle-class lifestyle, with social values that appear very similar to the world presented in Ibsen's play. A comfortable, clean and attractive home is as important, judging from this advertisement, as it was in 1879.

It would be easy to conclude that little has changed since Ibsen's day. However, there are some subtle but important differences. The woman in the advertisement is not presented as entirely powerless as Nora is, although her power is limited to the domestic field. It is also essential to consider genre, audience and purpose. An advertisement has a very different purpose to a literary text. The best literary texts challenge our view of the world and invite us to question what is around us; advertising, on the other hand, is designed to make us feel that the possession of one particular item would give us access to an ideal world where we would be totally happy. A comparison between Ibsen and this advertisement illustrates this.

Ibsen was questioning the role of women within his society because he wanted everyone to live a fulfilled and authentic life; Magnet Kitchens want everyone to buy their product. Ibsen was an individual at odds with his society and representing his anxieties in literary form; this advertisement is authored anonymously by an advertising agency and is designed to appeal to a particular readership linked to the magazine *Good Housekeeping*.

The language also reflects its context as a twenty-first-century text, as opposed to a nineteenth-century one. There are **minor sentences** without an initial capital letter, a particular feature of advertising. The text uses **contractions**, informality is implied by the use of pronouns, the language is generally simple and a word is used that would have been unfamiliar to Ibsen because it developed in the twentieth century: 'ergonomic'. (The prefix 'ultra' may feel like a modern word, but this in fact developed in the nineteenth century.)

CHAPTER 2, EXERCISE 5

This text is a screenplay and is the result of a collaboration of several people (the six members of the Monty Python team). It would also only actually be read by a handful of real fans, most people's contact with it being through seeing and hearing the film. This is addressed in the screenplay (in the same way as Ibsen's stage directions in chapter 1) by including detailed directions in italics to indicate the visual aspects of the film. There is also, like the Jackie Kennedy text, an intertextual reference, which in this case is to the film version of the stage musical, *Camelot*. Thus, the text's humour has a dual target: both the romantic notions of the Arthur legend and the film musical.

Like Twain's text, there is a continual mockery of the romantic ideal through the use of humour. Camelot is set up at the beginning of the extract as a wonderful place, described as 'amazing' and 'illuminated'. However, this opening is then undermined by Gawain who comments, 'It's only a model'. The simple, colloquial language that Gawain speaks to his page is contrasted with Arthur's elevated and pompous language, 'I bid you welcome'. Significantly, Gawain's undermining comment is made to a page, a character normally given little importance in the original legend (other than as a symbol of faithfulness). It is clear that many of the aristocratic values contained within the romantic myth are systematically mocked, fitting at a time when 'the establishment' was open to challenges from all sides during the 1970s.

The song in this extract is a **parody** of the songs that were included in the musical *Camelot*. The knights are presented as interested only in singing and dancing and the language creates comic juxtapositions through the use of rhyme (Camelot and Spam a lot). Spam is not conventionally viewed as the food of royalty and heroic knights do not typically sequin their vests. Even Arthur decides in the end, 'it is a silly place', perhaps retaining his dignity after all! The other target of the film is arguably those who unthinkingly consume the kind of ideologies represented in stage musicals such as *Camelot*, an interesting comparison with Jackie Kennedy's rather different response ten years earlier.

CHAPTER 3, EXERCISE 3

The most obvious representation of the power relations can be seen in the use of dialect. Elizabeth speaks in Standard English while Mary speaks in Scots dialect. Contrasts are immediately set up with the alternating speeches between the two characters. Lochhead presents Mary's language as much more poetic and evocative than Elizabeth's. Elizabeth's language is plain, 'strip her of her crown', and lacking in emotion. When she mentions feelings – 'I love my good cousin' – there is a hollow and insincere ring, almost as if she is trying to persuade herself. In reality, it appears as if she is trying to distance herself from her inevitable decision to execute Mary. Mary's language, on the other hand, is evocative, despairing and human. Her reflections on the reason for her love for Bothwell is to 'snuff oot the hale birlin' world in stillness'. As the audience knows that Mary is on the verge of her execution (and this knowledge creates **dramatic irony**), then this becomes even more poignant.

The contrast in language is at the heart of the contrast in character that Lochhead sets up. Both women are shown visually on the stage as isolated, but for very different reasons. Elizabeth has chosen her solitude and glories in it as the 'Virgin Queen'; Mary has had all those around her taken away from her in various ways and her need for human companionship has often left her vulnerable (there are implications of this in the mention of Bothwell). Elizabeth appears to be the wiliest politician and the final repetition of 'trick me' implies that she wants someone else to take responsibility for Mary's death; Mary appears to have been manipulated and used by others and is unable to extricate herself from her situation in spite of her ability to 'charm' men.

Lochhead's choice of the dramatic genre allows her to represent visually the power struggle between the two women – they are positioned on opposite sides of the stage. However, this is very evenly balanced and, although we know Elizabeth will be the political victor, the focus of the audience's empathy is Mary. Interestingly, Lochhead's twentieth-century perspective encourages her also to consider the women from a feminist perspective: both women are female sovereigns caught in a world where men are the conventional rulers. Lochhead notes in her stage directions that both women are alone 'but for those men and their paper and their pen'. Both women have been forced to make sacrifices: Elizabeth in becoming the 'Virgin Queen' and Mary, ultimately, in losing her life. The play can also be described as postmodern in the sense that, unlike Ibsen, Lochhead is not attempting to portray a realistic scene. The action has been stylised to become symbolic rather than literal and this is true of the play as a whole where each section shifts through a kaleidoscopic whirl of action and imaginary scenes from history reinterpreted for a modern audience.

CHAPTER 4, EXERCISE 4

Both texts are written in third person narrative and both made extensive use of humour. Both texts also primarily use direct speech or dialogue which adds drama and immediacy to the events and enhances the humour by showing the interactions of the characters. However, both texts handle their material in very different ways using very different narrative perspectives.

The Thackeray text has no Indian characters but has an English family as its main focus, one of whom has a position with the East India Company and has direct experience of living in India. He has returned with an appetite for curry and his mother has attempted to create an authentic dish for him. The humour in this passage is created by Becky's ignorance about curry and Indian spices. It is also clear that her intention is not to experience another culture but to curry favour (no **pun** intended) with Joseph Sedley who is unmarried. She turns an 'appealing' look to Joseph and is sure that everything that comes from India must be good. This is contrasted with the vulgarity of the Sedley family: Joseph is described as 'red' from 'gobbling' and his father is described as a 'coarse man' from the 'Stock Exchange'. The commercial world provides a backdrop for the family. The humour is further intensified by Becky's misunderstanding of the word chilli, believing it to be something cooling (a pun). In the end, she is reduced to begging for water and Mr Sedley sends his servant, Sambo, off to fetch some. India is portrayed here, through its food, as unromantic and comically dangerous for those unacquainted with its customs. Those involved in commercial relations, such as Joseph Sedley, are portrayed as greedy and vulgar but capable. The narrative perspective is solely from the view of the coloniser and the closest we get to a non-English character is the silent and obedient Sambo. Power very clearly and unproblematically resides with the English characters, particularly the Sedley family at the heart of the extract. However, their vulgarity and bad manners may make the reader doubt whether they will be capable of keeping this power – and the rest of the novel extends this idea further.

Zadie Smith's extract is very different. The narrative perspective here is the complete opposite. Food remains the prime focus and again we see English people interested in extending their knowledge of foreign customs by visiting an Indian restaurant. However, this time the Indian characters hope to make money from this and the commercial gain has been completely reversed. The same concerns appear, i.e. that English people are ill-equipped to deal with the rigours of hot curry. However, here it will be used for commercial profit. Humour is created by the technique of having the experienced owner, Ardashir, questioning the new recruit, Ravind, about what to do. Power resides with the Indian owner and waiters and we find humour in their strategies to earn more money.

CHAPTER 5, EXERCISE 5

The first major difference from classical tragedy is that both of these texts are novels written in prose. This immediately challenges traditional notions of literary superiority where poetry and poetic drama are often seen as intrinsically more serious and worthy than prose novels.

The Hardy text was written at the end of the nineteenth century at a time when social class and gender distinctions were changing. Hardy's choice of a working-class woman as his tragic hero is central for this (and akin to Ibsen's choice, although Ibsen chose to focus primarily on the middle classes). Critics have described the novel as a tragedy for later-Victorian England. It is expressed in novel form because this was the main literary focus for that age, just as poetic drama was the main focus for the Ancient Greeks and the Elizabethans. Thus, tragedy has been updated to make it relevant for a contemporary audience. The 'President of the Immortals' represents an uncaring and inevitable Fate, symbolised in the 'black flag', which human beings can only combat with friendship and love (symbolised in the holding hands of those witnessing it). Like previous tragic heroes, Tess is caught inevitably in a spiral of events that lead to her death; she shares the common lot of humanity which is to suffer and endure. At the end, there is loss but also a sense of renewal in these two characters who leave hand in hand.

Things Fall Apart was written in 1958 by a Nigerian writer at a time just prior to Nigeria's independence in 1960. The novel looks back to the time of the writer's own grandfather when white settlers were just beginning to arrive. The central character, Okonkwo, is a product of this African culture who, unlike many of his friends and family, refuses to submit to the new way of life. This, ultimately, becomes his tragedy and he, like Willy Loman in *Death of a Salesman*, is led to suicide. The tragedy is played out against an inevitable clash of two opposing cultures (symbolised here by the difficulty in burying Okonkwo). The novel itself reflects this clash: while there is considerable focus on the characteristics of Igbo (Okonkwo's tribe) culture, it is also written in English. Here, tragedy is updated to focus on a culture that both challenges and extends traditional western concepts of tragedy.

REFERENCES

Beard, A. (2001) *Texts and Contexts*, London: Routledge.

Beard, A. (2003) *The Language of Literature*, London: Routledge.

Carter, R. and McRae, J. (2001) *The Routledge History of Literature in English*, London: Routledge.

Eaglestone, R. (2000) *Doing English*, London: Routledge.

Jacobs, R. (2001) *A Beginner's Guide to Critical Reading*, London: Routledge.

Montgomery, M., Durant, A., Mills, S., Fabb, N. and Furniss, T. (2000) *Ways of Reading*, London: Routledge.

Pope, R. (2002) *The English Studies Book*, London: Routledge.

GLOSSARY

Listed below are the key terms used in the book, together with brief definitions.

Accent The way in which speakers from specific regional or social groups pronounce words. See also **dialect**

Address term Term used in speech to address another person, often conveying the level of formality, e.g. sir, mate

Allegorical, allegory Describing a narrative that has a deeper meaning than that presented on the surface

Allusion An indirect reference to an idea or theme taken from one work to another. The author usually relies on the fact that the reader will recognise this allusion

Anachronism, anachronistic Something not placed in its correct historical period. This may occur in error or intentionally to create humour

Anti-hero A central figure without the traditional heroic qualities

Archaism (or archaic) Use of language that is old-fashioned or obsolete

Blank verse Unrhymed iambic pentameter, the conventional verse form of Elizabethan drama

Borrowing A process whereby words are assimilated into a language from a foreign language

Canon A body of works agreed by various authorities to have sufficient literary merit to warrant further study. These works are often considered 'classics' and are perceived by many as fundamentally different from works produced within popular culture which have been traditionally seen to have less literary merit

Catharsis The release from tension that is supposedly experienced by an audience when watching a tragedy

Cliché An over-familiar, conventional expression

Colloquialism Informal language used in an everyday context. Demotic language is also the language spoken by ordinary people

Comedy Hard to define precisely. Generally, a work that ends optimistically and may use humour. Sub-genres are numerous

Connotations The range of associations that surround a word, as opposed to that word's dictionary definition or its denotation

Contractions Shortened forms of phrases, such as when 'it is' becomes 'it's', normally a feature of informal spoken language

Deconstruct(ion) A critical approach that emerged in the second half of the twentieth century which involves the close reading of texts but, unlike practical criticism, it seeks to tease out the inconsistencies and conflicts in these works rather than impose a coherent whole

Dialect A way of speaking in which grammatical structures and/or vocabulary identify the regional or social origin of the speaker. See also **accent**

Dialogue The conventions used to represent actual speech in literary texts. Also called direct speech. If the speaker is not named, the speech is called unattributed

Direct speech See **Dialogue**

Discourse This term has accumulated a range of definitions over the last few years. On a simple level, it means the laws governing spoken language. However, in this book it is used in its more theoretical sense to refer to the fact that all human knowledge is categorised in different ways, ultimately through language. This has created a range of different discourses. These discourses may be governed by a dominant ideology. For example, a legal discourse uses very specific vocabulary designed only to be understood by the educated few which immediately grants it greater social power

Dramatic irony Something in a play that the audience understand the significance of whereas the characters are unaware

Etymology The ways in which words change their meanings over time

Genre and sub-genre Genre refers to an identifiable text-type. It can be used in a number of ways: to identify a type of writing as in a report, a letter, a poem;

and it can identify a group of texts which have subject-matter in common as in crime fiction, travel writing, sports writing. Sub-genre is a branch of a genre, so if the genre is crime fiction, then police procedural is a sub-genre

Grammatical, grammar   The system that governs the way language is constructed. Grammatical terminology has been used in the analytical passages of this book and it is assumed that students will have an understanding of terms such as adjective, verb, pronoun, etc. There are numerous grammar guides available to develop this understanding further

Graphology   The visual aspects of a text, e.g. graphics, fonts, emboldening

Iambic metre   See **Metre**

Identity   The way individuals achieve a sense of themselves reflected in language through distinct forms such as accent and dialect

Ideology   A set of beliefs common to a social or historical group that seems natural or common-sensical. Historical criticism has often focused on the ways ideologies are represented in literary texts

Imperative   Sentence in the form of a command

Interrogative   Sentence in the form of a question

Intertextual(ity)   The notion that texts often show connections or influences from each other. There are many ways of showing intertextuality: direct quotation, allusion or parody being but three

Jargon   The specialised language of a professional group, e.g. computing

Juxtaposition   Something placed alongside something else to draw out an effective comparison or contrast

Lexis   The study of words in a text

Metre   Regular rhythmic patterns in poetry. The most common is iambic with its series of unstressed and stressed syllables

Minor sentence   A grammatically incomplete sentence without a main verb, often used in advertising

Narrative voice   The 'voice' that tells the story in a text. A simple distinction is between third person (he/she/it) and first person (I), although there are many further differences that can be established

Parody   An imitation of a work intended to ridicule

Phonetic   See **Phonological**

Phonological, phonology   Aspects of the sound system of a language. The system for categorising sounds is called phonetics

Postmodernism   A very broad term used to describe a range of experimental texts produced during the second half of the twentieth century. These texts typically focus on the meaninglessness of life, defy established literary conventions and play games with the reader

Practical criticism   A way of approaching literary analysis that became popular during the first half of the twentieth century. Its method is to focus on a close reading of a literary text, looking at the writer's style and language, and from this to express the critic's reaction to the work. There is no consideration of external factors such as the text's historical or social context

Problem play   A play that explores a contemporary social or moral problem. It has also been used, particularly with Shakespeare, to refer to a play that is difficult to categorise by using conventional labels such as tragedy or comedy

Propaganda   Texts devoted to the spreading of a particular idea or belief system

Pun   A play on words

Received pronunciation   The high-prestige accent associated with Standard English

Represent(ation)   The use of something to stand for something else. In literary and language study, this acknowledges that texts stand for the reality they represent rather than give direct and unprejudiced access to it

Rhyme   Words that are connected with similar sounds. This can be further subdivided into a range of rhyming techniques. Two successive rhyming lines are called rhyming couplets

Satire   A comic work ridiculing stupidity

Semantic field   A group of words that are related in meaning through being connected in a certain context

Setting   The place where a text is set, often of significance both geographically and historically

Slang   An informal language shared by a particular group which often gives a sense of group membership and identity, e.g. medical slang

Sonnet   A fourteen-line poem subdivided into further types according to its rhyme scheme

Standard English   The dialect with the highest prestige in English society, usually associated with education, the law and government

Sub-genre   See **Genre**

Symbol(ic)   An image that stands for something much larger or more complex. Particular images may have a range of symbolic references, e.g. a rose

Syntactical, syntax   The way sentences are constructed

Tragedy   A serious play with a central focus on a character who suffers a personal reversal of fortune. *See chapter 5 for a more detailed discussion of this*

Unattributed   See **Dialogue**

Related titles from Routledge

Edited by **Angela Goddard**, Manchester Metropolitan University, UK and
Adrian Beard, University of Newcastle upon Tyne, UK.

The *Intertext* series has been specifically designed to meet the needs of
contemporary English Language Studies. The core book, *Working with Texts*,
is the foundation text that provides an introduction to language analysis. It
is complemented by a range of 'satellite' titles that provide students with
hands-on practical experience of textual analysis through special topics. They
can be used individually or in conjunction with *Working with Texts*.

Each *Intertext* satellite title is:

- highly interactive, offering a range of task-based activities both for class use
  and self study
- written in a clear, accessible, user-friendly style with a full glossary
- fully illustrated with a variety of real language texts: literary texts, memos,
  signs, advertisements, leaflets, speeches, conversations

Available at all good bookshops
For ordering and further information on the Intertext series please visit:
www.routledge.com/rcenters/linguistics/series/intertext.html